lonely planet KIDS

A KID'S GUIDE TO
ROME

LET THE ADVENTURE BEGIN!

by Alexa Ward

Project Editor: Priyanka Lamichhane
Designers: John Foster, Andrew Mansfield
Publishing Director: Piers Pickard
Publisher: Rebecca Hunt
Art Director: Emily Dubin
Print Production: Nigel Longuet

The Lonely Planet Kids Travel Guides series is produced in partnership with the WonderLab Group, LLC.

Special thanks to our city consultant, Abigail Blasi, and editor, Rose Davidson.

Published in May 2025 by Lonely Planet Global Limited
CRN: 554153
ISBN: 9781837585267
www.lonelyplanet.com/kids
© Lonely Planet 2025
10 9 8 7 6 5 4 3 2 1
Printed in Malaysia

All rights reserved. No part of this publication may be reproduced, stored in a retrieval system or transmitted in any form by any means, electronic, mechanical, photocopying, recording or otherwise except brief extracts for the purpose of review, without the written permission of the publisher. Lonely Planet and the Lonely Planet logo are trademarks of Lonely Planet and are registered in the US Patent and Trademark Office and in other countries.

Although the author and Lonely Planet have taken all reasonable care in preparing this book, we make no warranty about the accuracy or completeness of its content and, to the maximum extent permitted, disclaim all liability from its use.

STAY IN TOUCH
lonelyplanet.com/contact

Lonely Planet Office:
IRELAND
Digital Depot, Roe Lane (off Thomas St),
Digital Hub, Dublin 8, D08 TCV4, Ireland

Paper in this book is certified against the Forest Stewardship Council™ standards. FSC™ promotes environmentally responsible, socially beneficial and economically viable management of the world's forests.

lonely planet KIDS

A KID'S GUIDE TO
ROME

LET THE ADVENTURE BEGIN!

by Alexa Ward

CONTENTS

- How to Use This Book — 10
- Welcome to Rome! — 12
- Mapping It Out — 14
- Getting Around Town — 20
- Places to Play — 32
- What a View! — 46
- Let's Eat! — 58
- A Hub of History — 70
- Modern Marvels — 82
- The Wild Side — 94
- Going Green — 106
- Secrets of the City — 118
- What's the Difference? — 130
- Index — 134
- Resources — 138
- Credits — 139

IMAGE: Cycling toward the Colosseum.

8   A Kid's Guide to ROME

How to Use This Book

Are you in search of a city's most delish desserts or wild about urban wilderness? Maybe you want to check out some places to play or discover the history and mysteries of the city. Or, perhaps, all of the above? Each chapter of this book has a unique theme. You can read the book from beginning to end or dip in and out! Don't forget to scour each page for fun facts, places, people, and more. Here are some highlighted features in the book.

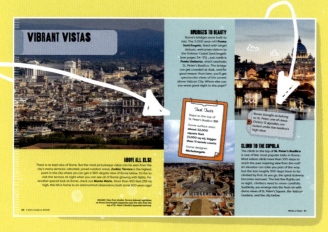

Like collecting facts and stats?

Check these out.

Here are a few translations for phrases you will find in the book.

ENGLISH / ITALIAN

Hello / Ciao
Goodbye / Arrivederci
Thank-you! / Grazie!
Let's go! / Andiamo!
That's fun! / É divertente!

What makes this city tick?

Look for "A Hub of History" on pages 70–81 or "Modern Marvels" on pages 82–93.

Curious about the weirdest, wackiest, and most unheard-of spots?

"Secrets of the City" is on pages 118–129.

Need something to do while waiting for the train, bus, plane, or car?

Look for "What's the Difference?" on pages 130–133.

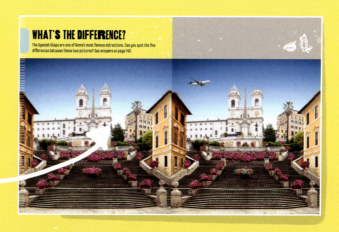

WELCOME TO ROME!

Behold, the Eternal City! Here, cobblestones line the ancient streets that once carried chariots through town. Rising from the banks of the Tiber River, Rome rolls across the landscape with its seven famous hills.

In the heart of the city, Centro Storico is packed with history at every turn. Visit the Colosseum, where gladiators once dueled. Make a wish as you toss a coin into the famous Trevi Fountain. At night, make your way around the city's many piazzas. In Rome, you'll find all this and much more. Your adventure begins now!

IMAGE: The Roman Forum.

THE ETERNAL CITY
The famous Roman poet Virgil, born in 70 BCE, called Rome an "empire without end." While Rome's empire eventually did collapse in 476 CE, the city survived and reinvented itself throughout some of the darkest times in human history. The nickname "the Eternal City" reflects the lasting Roman feeling that their city will endure forever.

Mapping It Out

VATICAN

CASTEL SANT'ANGELO

VILLA BORGHESE

PIAZZA NAVONA

PANTHEON

ORTO BOTANICO

TIBER RIVER

ST. PETER'S BASILICA

14   A Kid's Guide to Rome

BIOPARCO

CASINA DELLE CIVETTE

TREVI FOUNTAIN

MUSEUM OF ILLUSIONS

ROMAN FORUM

COLOSSEUM

ARCH OF CONSTANTINE

BATHS OF CARACALLA

Mapping It Out 15

REALLY, RIONI!

Rome was the first city ever to have a population of one million. Today, it is made up of 22 rioni (districts). Each neighborhood has its own coat of arms. Rome is also the only city in the world that has a whole other country inside it! Vatican City is the world's smallest country by both area and population. In Centro Storico (Historic Center), an area that spans several rioni, you'll find centuries of history everywhere you go. No matter where you are in Rome, there's lots to explore.

IMAGES: St. Peter's Square in Vatican City (below); the Farnese Gardens (opposite top); the Roman Forum (opposite bottom).

PRATI

VATICAN CITY

BORGO

CENTRO STORICO

Mapping It Out 17

Meet the Metro

Big red signs with the letter M mark the entrance to Rome's metro stations. Construction of the metro began in 1937, but World War II set things back for years. The first line was finally finished in 1955. Today, there are more than 70 stations and three train lines that run along 37 miles (60 km) of tracks all over the city. It may be Europe's smallest metro system, but it still takes riders to the top sights. Hop on!

Each of Rome's three metro lines can be identified by letter and color: A (orange), B (blue), and C (green).

18 A Kid's Guide to Rome

IMAGES: A metro train in a station (above); a sign marking a metro entrance (below); people standing in an underground metro station (opposite bottom).

Mapping It Out 19

GETTING AROUND TOWN

IMAGE: A view of the Colosseum.

ALL ROADS LEAD TO ROME

"Grab your walking shoes!" If you've heard this famous expression, you're already on your way to becoming an expert on one of the city's greatest legacies: its roads.

What's so special about a road? For ancient Romans, these paths—including early superhighways—made world-changing levels of connections, trade, and conquest possible. Roman road builders cleared land and laid each stone by hand—starting with the Via Appia, or Appian Way (see pages 74-75), in 312 BCE.

Today, when you travel the Eternal City's streets, you're navigating the same routes as early pilgrims and merchants, as well as the soldiers and noblemen that traveled by chariot and carriage. Need to rest your feet? Take a detour to the **Carriage Pavilion** at the Vatican Museums (see pages 78-79) to see some real-life examples of these old vehicles.

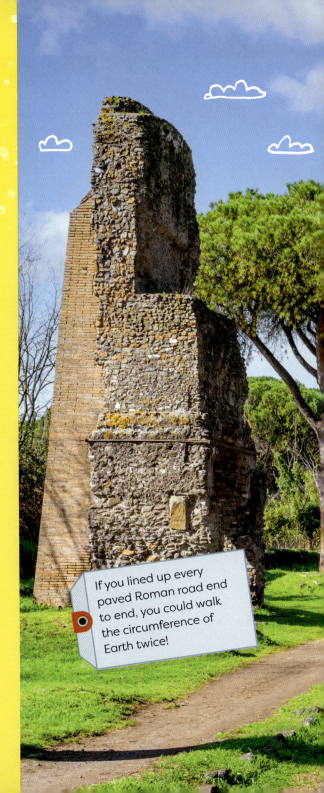

If you lined up every paved Roman road end to end, you could walk the circumference of Earth twice!

IMAGE: A person strolling on the Appian Way.

22   A Kid's Guide to ROME

A REAL MILESTONE

Measured at 1,000 paces or 5,000 Roman feet, the Roman *mille* (one thousand) laid the groundwork for the modern mile. Roman road builders installed pillars of stone along main roads, each carved with information that told travelers how far they'd come—which is how we got the term "milestone"!

ON WHEELS

IN THE ZONE

See that sign with the red circle? That's a Zona Traffico Limitado (ZTL), or Limited Traffic Zone. These are areas of the city where cars are not allowed in order to help reduce pollution and congestion. No cars also means it's easier for people to walk around, and Rome's historic streets and irreplaceable sites are protected from damage.

Traffic in ancient Rome once got so bad that Emperor Julius Caesar banned the use of horse-drawn carts from dawn to dusk.

TAXI, PLEASE!

Roman cab drivers use their local expertise to weave their white cars through the city's old, narrow streets—often including the ZTL zones, where they are usually an exception to the "no cars" rule. And there's no hailing required: passengers can get scooped up at taxi stops throughout the city. It can sometimes be a long wait—or maybe just long enough to grab gelato nearby?

BUSES ABOUND

Rome has more than 330 bus lines, and the buses are on the go from 5 a.m. until midnight. So what do people do between midnight and 5 a.m.? Well, the city has night buses, too! Twenty to be exact. When all other public transportation has come to a halt, these night buses, take over from midnight until the early hours of the morning. Rome's buses are the most widespread form of transportation in the city—there are 8,260 stops!

Before modern-day transportation, a journey from Rome to London could take about 157 days by oxcart.

ELECTRIC RIDES

Here's a fun way to get around: take an electric tuk-tuk or golf-cart tour and get up close to the city's most famous sites. You can choose what you'd like to see beforehand, so all your top spots are covered! The driver is also your tour guide and will tell you all about each spectacular site as you go. Enjoy a great ride while making new discoveries about the Eternal City!

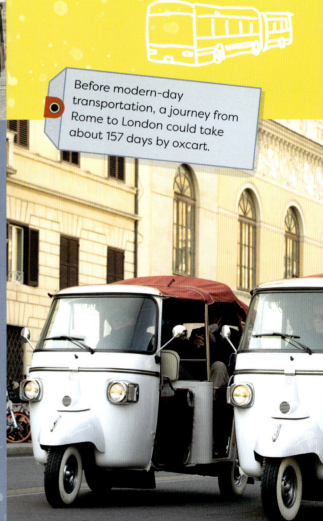

IMAGES: Public buses (above); electric tuk tuk (right); a ZTL street sign (opposite top); a line of Roman cabs (opposite bottom).

ALL ABOARD!

The Direttissima, Europe's first high-speed train, connects Florence and Rome. It travels at speeds of 155 miles per hour (250 km/h).

TAKE A TRAM

Rome's charming trams operate on six lines within the city. The tramlines don't run through the city center or hit many tourist hot spots. But if you want to discover some of Rome's other *rioni*, the tramway could be your chariot! The lovely and vibrant Trastevere neighborhood is a great place to be where the locals are. Check out the cobbled *vicoli* (small streets) and delicious pizzerias. Four trams converge at the Porta Maggiore. Here, you'll find one of the best preserved gates in the Aurelian Walls, which were built more than 2,000 years ago to defend Rome from invaders!

IMAGES: A Roman tram stopping in the Prati neighborhood (above); Termini station (opposite top); archaeological finds in an underground metro station (opposite bottom).

BEYOND THE METRO

Want to be whisked away to someplace beyond the metro's reach? The **Ferrovie Urbane**, or Urban Railway, is the way to go. Take the Roma-Lido line, also known as Metromare, which carries 90,000 people a day—many of whom head to the seaside neighborhood of Lido di Ostia for a refreshing dip.

Fast Facts

Metro length:
37 miles (60 km)

Number of metro lines: **3**

Busiest metro stop: **Termini**

UNDER CONSTRUCTION

For all its grandeur, Rome has one of the smallest underground metro systems in Europe. The city isn't well suited for subterranean tunnels. Why? Construction workers keep unearthing ruins while they're digging. The discoveries need to be treated with great care, slowing down construction. During construction of a new line in 2013, crews found an entire house 40 feet (12 m) underground! It once belonged to a military commander. On the plus side, some of the artifacts make their way into the system's design. The walls of the San Giovanni station are lined with a stone bathtub, peach pits, and coins found on the job.

Getting Around Town 27

TRAVEL BY FOOT

ETERNAL POSSIBILITIES

Spend a full day walking the streets of Rome and you'll tour thousands of years of history, art, and culture. Stroll the Appian Way (see pages 74–75). Conduct an ancient aqueduct scavenger hunt. Venture into shadowy cathedrals to seek out hidden masterpieces. Don't forget to pause at a piazza for some refreshing *acqua frizzante* (sparkling water) as you make your way through this urban maze. Just remember to offer up some coins to a fountain for luck.

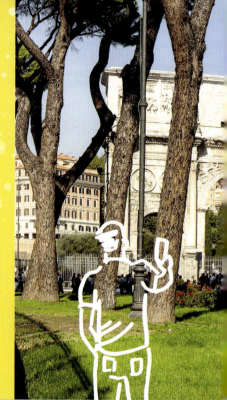

According to legend, Jesus Christ is said to have climbed the 28 steps of the Scala Sancta—about a half-hour walk from Piazza del Campidoglio—on the day of his death.

AN UPHILL CLIMB

Walking Rome doesn't just mean walking around, but also walking *up, up, up*. Prepare your leg muscles for an array of slopes to ascend and towers and steps to climb. Each incline is unique and comes with its own slice of history—like the **Piazza del Campidoglio** steps, which were designed by Michelangelo to be wide enough for horse traffic!

IMAGES: The Arch of Constantine (above); the steps of Piazza del Campidoglio (left).

Getting Around Town 29

UNUSUAL RIDES

MAKE VROOM!

From popemobiles to two-wheeled chariots, many kinds of vehicles have graced the streets of Rome throughout history. Today, you might notice some tinier transport. Locals often drive tiny vehicles like the iconic MINI Cooper or vintage Fiat 500s, as well as newer electric models that can barely seat two people. Also look out for the mini three-wheeled trucks with flatbeds that are used to make deliveries, often for fresh produce. These are the Piaggio Ape, named for their buzzing sounds (*ape* means "bee"). The Italian postal service even uses a version of these to whiz through the city's labyrinth.

THE POPEMOBILE

How does the pope greet large crowds? Papal attendants once carried him through the streets on a chair called the *sedia gestatoria*. It has been replaced with the popemobile, a specially designed car, truck, or jeep.

The Piaggio Museum in northern Italy has more than 350 motorbike models on display.

30 A Kid's Guide to ROME

VESP—AAH

Whoosh. What was that colorful blur over your shoulder? Motorbikes are everywhere in Rome, but none are more closely connected with the city than the Vespa (Italian for "wasp"). Invented in Italy, the iconic moped has a fascinating history. World War II left Italian roads in shambles, making passage difficult for normal cars. People needed an effective way to travel while rebuilding after the war. A former plane manufacturer created the scooter to solve the problem.

IMAGES: People enjoying a mini car (above); a classic Vespa (left).

PLACES TO PLAY

IMAGE: People splashing in a water park just an hour outside of central Rome.

WIDE-OPEN SPACES

FORTRESS OF FUN

Stone angels beckon visitors to the imperial fortress of **Castel Sant'Angelo**. Originally built as a tomb for Emperor Hadrian, it became a prison, then a fortress. Here, you can explore the castle bastions, shadowy passages, and rows of cannons that once protected the building from invaders. Castel Sant'Angelo is encircled by the approximately 12-acre (5-ha) Parco Adriano, which has a playground so you can act out the dramatic battles that once raged here—or you can just use the swings!

The Baths of Caracalla also included a public library on the grounds.

The *Passetto di Borgo* is a secret passageway that connects the Vatican to Castel Sant'Angelo, which was once a fortress for the pope.

Fast Facts
Year built: **139 CE**

Number of emperors' ashes inside: **9**

Passetto length: **2,625 feet (800 m)**

SCRUB-A-DUB-DUB

The astounding ruins of the **Baths of Caracalla** are a reminder of how important bathing was in Roman culture. This thermal bath complex had two *palaestrae* (gyms), a *frigidarium* (cold room), a *tepidarium* (medium room), a *caldarium* (hot room), dressing rooms, and many more spaces for socializing and relaxing. You can't bathe here anymore, but you can grab VR (virtual reality) headsets to see how the grounds would have looked in ancient times! The baths could accommodate 1,600 bathers and were used for more than 300 years!

IMAGES: Entering Castel Sant'Angelo (above); the ruins of the Baths of Caracalla (left).

PLAYFUL PIAZZAS

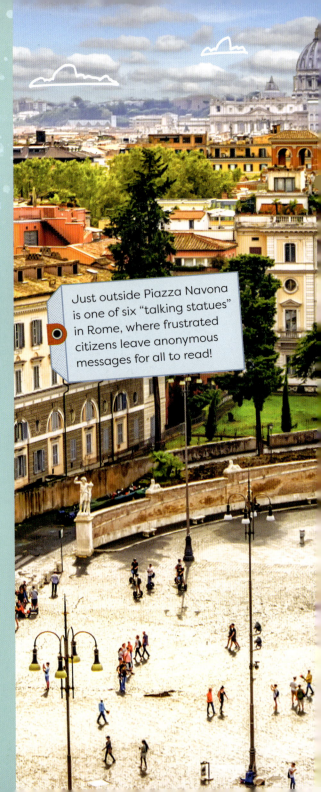

The piazza, or public square, is a building block of Roman culture. Known in ancient times as "forums," piazzas have been centers of shopping, worship, and culture for centuries. The **Piazza del Popolo** (the People's Square) is Rome's most popular square and was designed in the 16th century as the city's main northern entrance. The massive Flaminio Obelisk, one of 13 ancient Egyptian pillars that can be found in the city, rises from the center of the square. Here, you can see people acting as "living" statues or bubble blowers entertaining the crowds. From nearby **Pincian Hill**, you can view the bustle of the all the people below.

The lively **Piazza Navona**, another popular spot, was built on top of an ancient stadium where Romans watched gymnastic competitions. On any given day, you might see street performers, musicians, and even fire-eaters! Along the square, don't miss the fairies, goblins, and dolls of **Al Sogno**. The toy store has been around for more than 75 years.

Just outside Piazza Navona is one of six "talking statues" in Rome, where frustrated citizens leave anonymous messages for all to read!

IMAGE: A view of Piazza del Popolo.

36 A Kid's Guide to ROME

AN EVENING STROLL

Piazzas are the heart of an Italian tradition—the *passeggiata*, or evening stroll. Under the setting sun, the city's squares start to fill with friendly chatter and laughs from people gathering together. Take your own stroll and join the fun!

Fast Facts

Capacity of Piazza del Popolo: **65,000+ people**

Height of obelisk: **85 feet (26 m)**

Height of obelisk with cross: **117 feet (36 m)**

MAGNIFICENT MUSEUMS

WHERE KIDS RULE

Explora, Rome's children's museum, is located in an old bus depot that dates back to 1877. Today, the building is brimming with interactive activities like the *Valuable Plastics* exhibit where you can transform plastic waste into new objects using a 3D printer. More than 140,000 people a year visit Explora to climb, create, and enjoy all the fun!

MASTERFUL MACHINES

Experience the genius of Leonardo da Vinci firsthand at the **Museo Mostra di Leonardo**. The museum has more than 60 interactive inventions—each brought to life from his notebooks—including wooden tanks, crossbows, and a pair of giant wings designed for human flight. High-tech holograms give a unique look at how everything works. Leave with a genius idea of your own!

38 A Kid's Guide to ROME

ICONIC IKONO

Next to the Pantheon temple (see page 72) is the ultramodern **IKONO Roma**. There are no frescoes or statues here—but there is a ball pit! Step inside to be swept away by neon light art, swirling colors, and lots of confetti. The immersive experience lasts about one hour, making IKONO a great place to take a break from the weather or let out some extra energy.

> At the archaeological ruins of Palazzo Valentini, you can tour an ancient Roman house through projections and headphones.

A WONDROUS WELCOME

Get an official greeting from the city at **Welcome to Rome**. This incredible account of the history of Rome is an excellent first stop on your visit. Sit back in a cozy cinema to watch a 4D movie that projects onto the walls, floor, and ceiling. The immersive video brings 2,700 years of history to life before your eyes—in only 30 minutes!

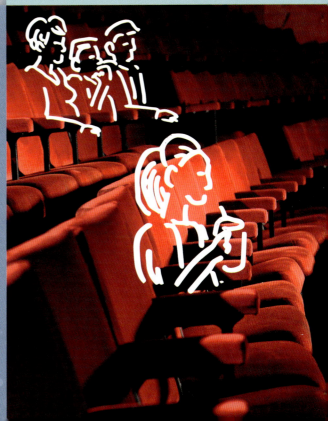

IMAGES: A person sinking into a ball pit (above); a row of empty theater seats (right); a child playing at Explora (opposite top); Leonardo da Vinci drawing (opposite bottom).

MAKE A SPLASH

WILD WAVES

Rome's love for water is on full display at **Hydromania**, a water park on the western outskirts of the city. This water park has multiple swimming areas—including a nearly-Olympic-size pool! There are also high-rise waterslides, a wave pool, "spin bowls," and many more watery attractions that offer every kind of thrill, from relaxing to raging. See water gush from Mermaid Rock in the center of the lagoon or interact with Jimmy the Fish, a colorful character that dumps big buckets of water from overhead—watch out!

Fast Facts

Number of attractions: **20+**

Number of waterslides: **6**

Splash zone size: **26,900 square feet (2,500 sq m), over twice the size of an Olympic-size pool**

Fast Facts
Number of seasonal visitors: **220,000**

Number of waterslides: **8**

Largest pool: **82 feet by 39 feet (25 m by 12 m)**

GET YOUR TICKET!

Step into a fairy tale at Rome's main amusement park, **LunEur**. Classic rides like a twisty caterpillar roller coaster and spinning teacups are only the beginning of the whimsical adventure. Can you spot the dome of St. Peter's Basilica from the top of the Ferris wheel? The park—also called the Garden of Wonders—changes every season, with spooky Halloween-themed attractions in the fall and ice-skating in the winter. Of course, it wouldn't be authentically Roman without a few water features—like the summertime splash zone and suds pit!

LunEur is the oldest amusement park in Italy.

IMAGES: Visitors enjoying a water park in Rome (above); a bird's-eye view of LunEur (left).

Places to Play 41

READY TO RACE!

TAKE YOUR MARKS

The four stadiums of **Foro Italico** await you in this sprawling sports complex. Tennis fans will love sitting courtside at Stadio Centrale. Just a jaunt away is Stadio Olimpico del Nuoto, or Olympic Swimming Stadium. Built for the 1960 Summer Olympics, the aquatic arena has a tunnel where competitors emerged poolside in dramatic fashion! There's also Stadio dei Marmi, a running track where premier Italian athletes once trained. But the trophy belongs to Stadio Olimpico, a soccer (or football as it's known in Europe and other parts of the world) stadium that can sit 70,000 screaming fans!

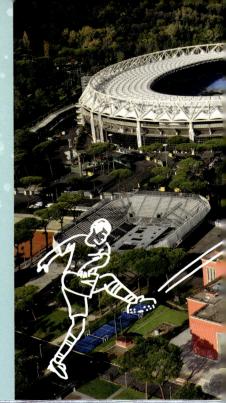

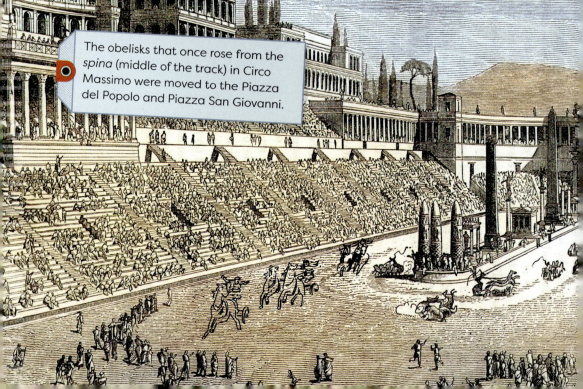

The obelisks that once rose from the *spina* (middle of the track) in Circo Massimo were moved to the Piazza del Popolo and Piazza San Giovanni.

The Foro Italico has hosted the Olympics, the World Cup, and the World Aquatics Championships.

CIRCUS OF CHARIOTS

This isn't your average circus! **Circo Massimo** (Circus Maximus) was once the largest racecourse in Rome, holding up to 250,000 people—four times the Colosseum's capacity! Now it's also the city's oldest arena, built nearly 600 years before the Colosseum. In the arena's heyday, horse-drawn chariots whizzed past cheering spectators. Now you can climb the arena's medieval tower or run the racetrack!

IMAGES: *The Foro Italico from above (above); an historic illustration of Circo Massimo (left).*

Places to Play 43

TOTALLY TIBER

Fast Facts

Length of island: **890 feet (271 m)**

Width of island: **220 feet (67 m)**

Bridges to the mainland: **Ponte Cestio, Ponte Fabricio**

The Ponte Fabricio, which leads to Tiber Island, is considered the oldest bridge in Rome. Most of it has been standing for more than 2,000 years!

LAND AHOY!

The history of the small island of **Isola Tiberina** (Tiber Island) is teeming with myths and legends—like the story that it was formed after furious Romans threw a tyrant's wheat into the river. Or the story of a legendary boat trip that inspired early Romans to construct the island into the shape of a ship complete with an obelisk "mast"! This tiny island is only about three soccer fields long. For thousands of years, it was where people went to get better when they were sick. Many thought the well in the island's thousand-year-old church contained miraculous healing waters.

IMAGES: The "prow" of Tiber Island (above); diners eating al fresco in the Jewish Quarter (opposite top); a line of vendors during Lungo il Tevere (opposite bottom).

44 A Kid's Guide to ROME

HISTORY HAVEN

Rome's Jewish population is among the oldest in Europe. The **Jewish Quarter**, found between the Tiber River and Piazza Venezia, is full of bakeries and restaurants that serve mouth-watering dishes—like *pizza ebraica* (a raisin-studded pastry), fried artichokes (see page 65), and a wild cherry and ricotta *crostata*—some of which are found nowhere else in the world! Here, you can also visit Tempio Maggiore (the Great Synagogue), built more than 120 years ago.

ALONG THE TIBER

The annual **Lungo il Tevere** summer festival is held along the banks of the Tiber River from June to September—thus its name, which means "along the Tiber"! The open-air festival is full of games, music, theater performances, artisans, and mounds of sizzling street food. To cool down, have a *grattachecca*: shaved ice with fruit toppings (see page 69). Here, most events are held in the evening for some nighttime fun!

Places to Play 45

WHAT A VIEW!

IMAGE: Sunrise on St. Peter's Basilica.

THRILLING HILLS

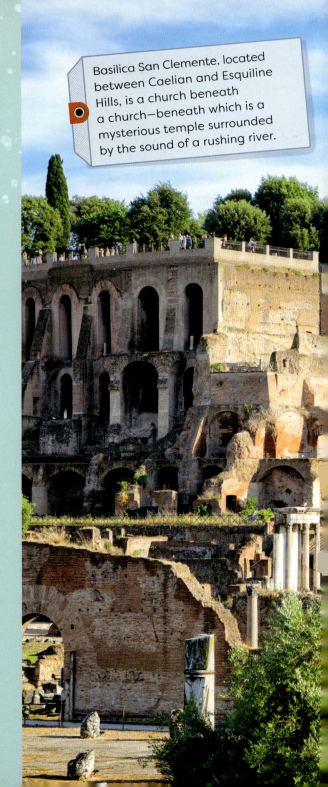

Basilica San Clemente, located between Caelian and Esquiline Hills, is a church beneath a church—beneath which is a mysterious temple surrounded by the sound of a rushing river.

Just east of the Tiber River, a handful of hills—named Aventine, Caelian, Capitoline, Esquiline, Palatine, Quirinal, and Viminal—huddle together. These are the *Sette Colli di Roma* (Seven Hills of Rome). The ancient city rose from these gently curving forms, making them an essential part of Rome's history and culture.

Every hill is like a living museum, each with unique wonders. **Esquiline Hill** has an epic view of the Colosseum, while **Capitoline Hill** is home to steeply sloping ancient gardens and Michelangelo's Piazza del Campidoglio (see pages 28–29). Then there's **Palatine Hill**, where—according to myth—twin brothers Romulus and Remus founded Rome in 753 BCE. Today, the hill holds a maze of treasures, including mural paintings (called frescoes) and Europe's first botanical gardens. Nearby are the ruins of the **Roman Forum**. Once a bustling hub of people and activity, the forum was the beating heart of the ancient empire.

IMAGES: *A view of Palantine Hill and the Roman Forum.*

48 A Kid's Guide to ROME

TWIN TROUBLE
According to myth, a local king ordered infant twin brothers Romulus and Remus to be abandoned because their claim to the throne threatened his rule. The twins were spared by the river god Tiberinus. They grew up and toppled the king and then set out to make their own city. Too bad they couldn't get along. According to legend, Romulus wanted to build on Palatine Hill, but Remus preferred Aventine. So Romulus killed his brother and founded the city—hence the name Rome.

At the start of the Roman Empire, Palatine Hill was home to the emperor's palace. This is where we got the word "palace"!

VIBRANT VISTAS

ABOVE ALL ELSE

There is no bad view of Rome. But the most picturesque vistas can be seen from the city's many terraces—elevated, paved outdoor areas. **Zodiac Terrace** is the highest point in the city where you can get a 360-degree view of Rome below. It's fun to visit the terrace at night when you can see all of Rome glowing with lights. For another special look at Rome, check out **Monte Mario**. More than 450 feet (138 m) high, this hill is home to an astronomical observatory built some 600 years ago!

IMAGES: View from Zodiac Terrace (above); nighttime at Ponte Sant'Angelo (opposite top); the view from the top of St. Peter's Basilica (opposite bottom).

BRIDGES TO BEAUTY

Rome's bridges were built to last. The 2,000 year-old **Ponte Sant'Angelo**, lined with angel statues, welcomes visitors to the fortress Castel Sant'Angelo (see pages 34–35). Just north is **Ponte Umberto**, which overlooks St. Peter's Basilica. The bridge can get crowded at dusk, and for good reason: from here, you'll get spectacular views of the sunset above Vatican City. Where else can you wave good night to the pope?

Fast Facts

Steps to the top of St. Peter's Basilica: **551**

Dome surface area: **about 32,000 square feet (3,000 sq m), bigger than 11 tennis courts**

Dome designer: **Michelangelo**

Bones thought to belong to St. Peter, one of Jesus Christ's 12 apostles, are buried under the basilica's high altar.

CLIMB TO THE CUPOLA

The climb to the top of **St. Peter's Basilica** is one of the most popular treks in Rome. Most visitors climb more than 500 steps to reach the awe-inspiring view from the roof! An elevator can take you part of the way, but the last roughly 300 steps have to be climbed by foot. As you go, the spiral stairway becomes narrower. The last few flights are so tight, climbers need to move carefully. Suddenly, you emerge into the fresh air with divine views of St. Peter's Square, the Vatican Gardens, and the city below.

What a View! 51

MARVELOUS MASTERPIECES

MEET GLADIATORS AND GODS

Here's a chance to mingle with Rome's bravest and boldest! The three buildings that make up the **Capitoline Museums** hold statues, tile mosaics, and loads of mythological figures. Greet the statue of Medusa, a monster with snakes for hair, or wave hello to a large bust of Emperor Constantine. Plus, see if you can spot the colossal sculpture of the emperor's foot!

Bernini, whose sculpture *David* portrayed David slaying Goliath, was said to have used his own face as a model.

MARBLE MAGIC

The **Galleria Borghese** is an essential pit stop for anyone looking to see epic statues and frescoes inspired by the heroes, beasts, and gods of Western mythology. The gallery is home to several of Gian Lorenzo Bernini's (see pages 92–93) amazingly lifelike statues. For a sneaky surprise, look to the highest corners of the museum's many rooms. You can see monster faces staring back at you!

52 A Kid's Guide to ROME

Museum Machine

Over the centuries, many Roman buildings have found new uses—including this modernized spot. **Centrale Montemartini** is an electrical power plant turned quirky museum. The sight of Greek and Roman marble statues standing among turbines, hulking diesel engines, and large boilers is a refreshing twist on ancient art. Don't skip this shrine to marble and metal.

> Centrale Montemartini has a restored 19th-century train that was designed as a popemobile for Pope Pius IX.

Treasure Hunting

If your neck hurts from craning to look up at statues, change gears and head to the **Palazzo Massimo alle Terme**. Along with its impressive mosaics, fresco-filled rooms, and bronze statues, the basement of this former palace is full of jewels and ancient Roman coins. Ancient coins were once like a form of social media: they were a way for emperors to advertise their image, wealth, and power to the masses.

IMAGES: A headless statue found in Centrale Montemartini (above); ancient Roman coins (right); antique busts inside the Capitoline Museums (opposite top); sculptures by Gian Lorenzo Bernini at Galleria Borghese (opposite bottom).

ART ON THE STREET

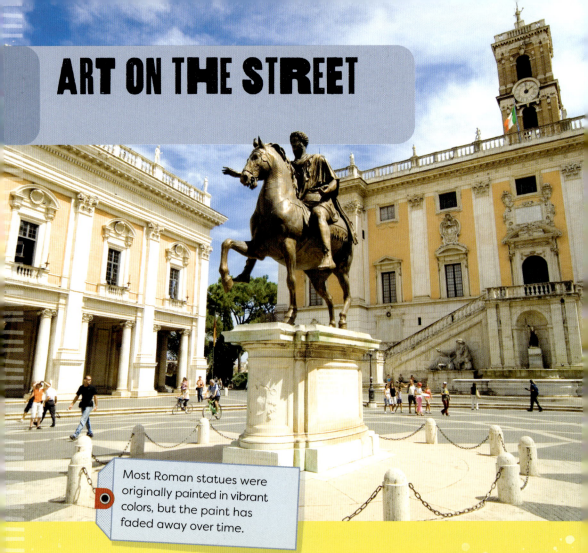

Most Roman statues were originally painted in vibrant colors, but the paint has faded away over time.

WALK OF FAME

Seek out the statues of some of the city's oldest icons while you stretch your legs. See if you can find former Roman emperor and philosopher Marcus Aurelias in Piazza del Campidoglio (see pages 28–29). Or look for former Roman general and self-proclaimed dictator Julius Caesar—known for shaking up the politics of the Roman Republic—in **Via dei Fori Imperiali**. There are rulers, artists, and religious leaders to greet around every piazza.

IMAGES: The statue of Marcus Aurelias in Piazza del Campidoglio (above); giant sandaled foot sculpture (opposite top); colorful art in the San Lorenzo neighborhood (opposite bottom).

54 A Kid's Guide to ROME

A GIANT FOOT

Hidden away in a small alley near the Pantheon, close to Via del Piè di Marmo (Marble Foot Way), there is a sculpture of a giant sandaled foot. At 4 feet (1.2 m) long, **Piè di Marmo** (Marble Foot) was once part of a larger statue that archaeologists believe was 25 feet (7.6 m) tall! In 1878, the foot was moved from Marble Foot Way to its current location because it was in the way of a funeral procession for King Emmanuel II.

ART ALL AROUND

For centuries, people have been leaving their mark on Rome, literally. Roman street art comes in all forms, from catacomb carvings to the most modern murals. Today, the neighborhood of **San Lorenzo** is the heart of the city's outdoor art. Take a street-art tour with a local guide or take an art class to make your own mosaics. Or download a free online map of the neighborhood art and discover this open-air museum on your own!

What a View! 55

UNDERGROUND ADVENTURE

EXPLORE THE CATACOMBS

Romans were forbidden from burying the dead within city limits, so what did they do? Built catacombs, of course! Outside the city limits, the **Catacombs of Rome** are intricate underground cemeteries with long tunnels, humble graves, and grand mausoleums. The tombs are spooky but fun to explore. These subterranean museums are known as important early Christian burial sites, which hold examples of religious art and ancient graffiti left behind by visiting pilgrims. Jewish and pagan tombs can be found within the tunnels, too. The catacombs are a cross section of the city's multicultural history.

Fast Facts

Number of distinct remains: **4,000**

Number of chambers: **6, including the crypt of the skulls, crypt of the pelvises, and crypt of the leg bones**

Fast Facts

Number of Roman catacombs: **60**

Number open to the public: **5**

Age of oldest catacomb: **over 2,000 years**

CHILLED TO THE BONE

Hidden underneath a Roman Catholic church on Via Veneto is one of the creepiest sites in Rome—an underground burial chamber filled with stacks of skulls, skeletons dressed in distinctive robes, and ceilings decorated with bone arrangements. The **Capuchin Crypt**—commonly called the "Bone Chapel"—was first built in the 1630s by Capuchin friars who moved to Rome to start a new order, bringing with them the remains of their dead. Why did they decide to turn those human remains into art? You can ponder the mystery as you look at the skeletal displays. It's thought that the church's friars would visit the crypt every evening to pray. What a bedtime ritual!

IMAGES: Visitors in the depths of the Catacombs of Rome (above); inside the Capuchin Crypt (left).

What a View! 57

LET'S EAT!

IMAGE: A child having lunch al fresco.

TASTY TRADITIONS

ON COURSE
A traditional Italian meal comes in several courses: aperitivo and antipasti (appetizers); *primo*, which usually includes pasta, risotto, or soup; and *secondo*, a dish centered around meat or a hearty vegetable. You don't have to eat *every* course, but don't forget the *dolce*—dessert!

Roasted mice and flamingo tongues were considered delicacies in ancient Rome.

OUTDOOR EATS

One of Rome's many culinary joys is dining *al fresco* . . . outside! Taking your carbonara (see page 62) on the sidewalk offers an incredible opportunity to people-watch, catch the sunset, or simply participate in lively Roman culture. Feel the city itself swirling around you while you swirl your bucatini (see page 63) on a fork. While in the Eternal City, take a pizza or pasta cooking class—why not get your hands dirty?

IMAGES: Kids playing near an outdoor café (above);
a traditional plate of coratella (opposite top);
pecorino romano (opposite bottom).

60   A Kid's Guide to ROME

MEATY MATH

Quinto quarto, or "fifth quarter," refers to the offal of animals—their organ meats. Centuries ago, nobles picked the best quarter, or part, of a butchered animal. Religious leaders got the second cut, merchants the third, and soldiers the fourth. Peasants created a rich cuisine from whatever was left over—including tripe, kidneys, tail, and more edible organs. Today, this *cucina povera* (peasant cooking) can be found in dishes like oxtail stew and *coratella* (lamb innards) with artichokes.

The ketchup of ancient Rome was garum, a sauce made from fermented fish meat, blood, and intestines.

Fast Facts

Amount of DOP pecorino produced per year: **30,000+ tons (27,000+ mt)**

Number of farms producing pecorino: **12,000**

Number of employees on farms: **25,000**

A CHEESY NOTE

The sharp, salty, crumbly *pecorino romano* is one of the oldest cheeses in the world. Because it aged well, was nutritious, and was easy to transport, this cheese was once part of a daily ration for soldiers known as the Roman legionaries. Like its cousin Parmesan, pecorino is easy to grate, making it the perfect cheese to sprinkle over dishes like *cacio e pepe* (see page 63). Today, authentic pecorino is still made according to its original recipe. (Look for the official "DOP" label, which guarantees that the cheese has been made according to tradition.)

Let's Eat! 61

THE PERFECT PASTA

Pepper was incredibly valuable in the ancient world. During the fall of Rome, one foreign general demanded 3,000 pounds (1,361 kg) of pepper in exchange for not attacking the city.

COME FOR THE CARBONARA

Fresh pasta, eggy sauce, pecorino cheese, salty pork, a few dashes of pepper—this is the magic spell for Roman carbonara. An authentic recipe requires guanciale, a type of pork that has been seasoned, cured (preserved), and aged. Some say carbonara was first made by American soldiers during World War II with their egg and bacon rations. Others say it was invented by a secret revolutionary society. The true origins of carbonara are a mystery, but there is no doubt it's one of modern Rome's tastiest delights.

IMAGES: A plate of carbonara (above); cacio e pepe (opposite top); bucatini all'amatriciana (opposite bottom).

CACIO LATER!

This dish of fresh pasta tumbled in pepper and grated pecorino is a symbol of Rome. *Cacio e pepe* (KAH-choh eh PEH-peh) likely came from shepherds who needed a hearty meal while moving their flocks. So they grabbed pecorino, black peppercorns, and dried spaghetti. Today, the dish can be found in restaurants on nearly every city street.

Fast Facts

Percentage of Italians who eat pasta daily: **20**

Average yearly pasta intake per adult: **51 pounds (23 kg)**

BRAVO, BUCATINI

Another simple but essential pasta dish is *bucatini all'amatriciana*, which combines tomatoes, pecorino, and guanciale (Italian pork) into a tornado of taste. When the pasta dish became popular in the 19th century, tomato sauce had only recently been invented by famous chef Francesco Leonardi—who is rumored to have served it to the pope. *Bucatini* means "little holes" in Italian; it's a thick, hollow spaghetti with, yes, a hole through the middle!

Let's Eat! 63

STREET FOOD

Many believe that Romans, without hearths to cook on at home, might have invented fast food with public hot-food counters called thermopolia.

SUPPLÌ IN DEMAND

A meal you can hold in your hand? Yes, please! *Supplì* are the pinnacle of Roman street food. The fried breadcrumb croquettes contain a melt-in-your-mouth combination of steaming rice, stringy mozzarella cheese, and savory sauce. Supplì were once fried on-the-go by vendors who carried large cauldrons of boiling oil through the streets. Today, the delicious balls can be found almost everywhere—but for a special treat browse the many choices at the historic **Testaccio Market** (see pages 110–111).

IMAGES: Classic *supplì* (above); stacks of typical porchetta *sandwiches* (opposite top); a close-up of frying artichokes (opposite bottom).

PORTABLE PORK

There are many ways to savor *porchetta*, or roasted pork, but the most on-the-go method comes in sandwich form. The *panino con porchetta* (roasted pork sandwich) is bursting with warm roasted meat, often seasoned with herbs and dripping with fat. Can you hear the crunch of perfectly toasted bread as you take a bite? Keep an eye out for other porchetta-topped street food items—like *porchetta pizza al taglio* (by the slice)!

The term *scarpetta* refers to the act of soaking up leftover sauce with bread. It's tradition!

FRIED "FLOWERS"

Jewish-style fried artichokes are a blend of flavor and textures. The flowerlike vegetable is deep-fried to be crunchy on the outside and soft on the inside, and then salted and spritzed with lemon. It was once sold only as street food within the Jewish Quarter—but now they are found on menus across the city, from the fanciest trattoria to the tiniest food stalls. Many say that the *carciofo Romanesco* (also called *cimarolo*), a local purple-and-green artichoke variety, makes for the best version. Snack away!

Let's Eat! 65

ICONIC EATERIES

FORMAL FOOD

Italy takes its food seriously, which is why eateries in Rome come in many different forms. The *ristorante* is the most formal type of restaurant, where diners will get a sit-down meal, a long menu, and a full waitstaff. For classic *cucina romana*, **La Campana** is the place to be. It has been serving food since 1518—that's more than 500 years! It claims to be the city's oldest restaurant!

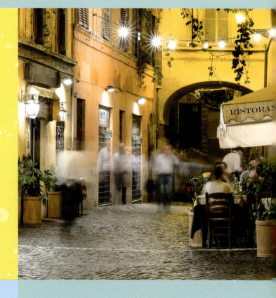

There are an estimated 2.7 billion pizzas made in Italy each year.

SLICES OF HEAVEN

At Rome's many pizzerias, you have your pick of everything from sauceless white slices to red tomato pies. The cheesy flatbread comes with a Roman twist—unlike Neapolitan pizza popular in the United States, the city's signature style of pizza has no true crust. Instead, the toppings reach all the way to the edge of the bread. Conduct your own taste test at local favorites like **Forno Renella** in Trastevere or **Forno da Milvio** in Monti, near the Colosseum.

SAVORY SANDWICHES

The *paninoteca* is a casual eatery that caters to one thing: making panini! A panini isn't just any sandwich—panini should be pressed and heated up to make the fillings extra gooey. The best paninotecas use local produce and freshly baked focaccias. For a modern twist, try a "pocket pizza"—a kind of handheld triangular sandwich—from **Trapizzino**. Chomp until you drop!

According to legend, Roman men used to propose to their beloved by hiding a ring in a maritozzo, a traditional cream-filled bun.

DARING DESSERTS

What's the point of dining without dessert? The *pasticceria* is your sweet spot—literally! For a bite of some history, grab a strawberry tart at the traditional, family-run **Regoli Pasticceria** in Centro Storico, or visit **Pasticceria il Boccione**, the Jewish Quarter's oldest bakery. Since 1815, it has been serving unique pastries, including *pizza ebraica*—a kind of bread encrusted with dried fruits and nuts.

IMAGES: A focaccia sandwich (above); the entrance to Regoli Pasticceria (right); a ristorante in Trastevere (opposite top); a slice of Roman pizza (opposite bottom).

SWEET TREATS

TEMPTING TIRAMISU

This divine cake is made with layers of biscotti called "ladyfingers," sugar-whipped eggs, and mascarpone cream. All is drowned in savory espresso and topped with a dusting of cocoa. Some bakers even add thin strawberry slices to their tiramisu (Italian for "pick me up") for an extra helping of sweetness. Sometimes tiramisu is made with traces of alcohol—check before ordering!

Stracciatella means "little rags." The name is used to describe three different types of Italian food: soup, cheese, and—of course—gelato!

GRAB A GELATO

Don't mistake this chilly treat for ice cream—gelato ("frozen" in Italian) is made with less butterfat and churned much more slowly than ice cream, giving it a creamier texture. Plus, it doesn't melt as quickly as ice cream! Rome is filled with *gelaterie*, but stop by the prize-winning **Neve Di Latte** for a scoop of traditional *stracciatella* (milky gelato with flakes of chocolate) or funkier flavors like sour cherry.

CREAM OF THE CROP

The English translation for *panna cotta* ("cooked cream") might not entice your taste buds, but names can be deceiving. Much like a somewhat firm pudding, the dessert is a mix of simple ingredients—cream, sugar, and gelatin—which give the substance a firm shape. Flavors like vanilla can be added or syrups made from *frutti di bosco* (berries) can be drizzled on top.

> Ancient Romans enjoyed cold desserts. Snow was often carried down from the surrounding mountains by *nevaroli* (snowmen) to feed the demand!

BEAT THE HEAT

If you're one of the millions of visitors who descend on Rome at summertime, grab some *grattachecca* for some relief from the blazing heat. To make the refreshing treat, a *grattacheccaro* scrapes ice from massive blocks with a tool called a *raschietto*, and then puts the shavings in a cup and pours fruit syrups or juices on top. Simple, old-fashioned grattachecca can be found at kiosks along the banks of the Tiber River. Just don't confuse it with the popular slushy treat *granita*—but do try them both!

IMAGES: *Panna cotta with fresh berries (above); an icy treat (right); a slice of tiramisu (opposite top); fruit-flavored gelato (opposite bottom).*

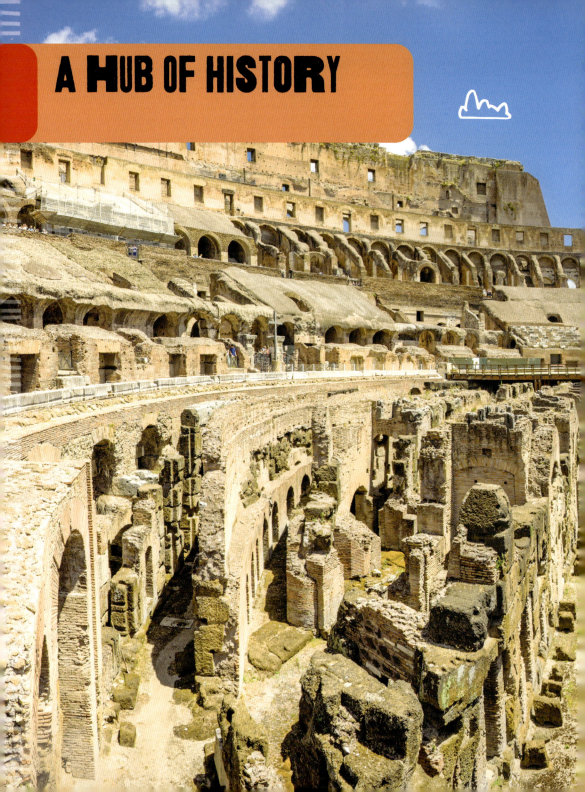

A HUB OF HISTORY

IMAGE: Inside the Colosseum.

TERRIFIC TRIO

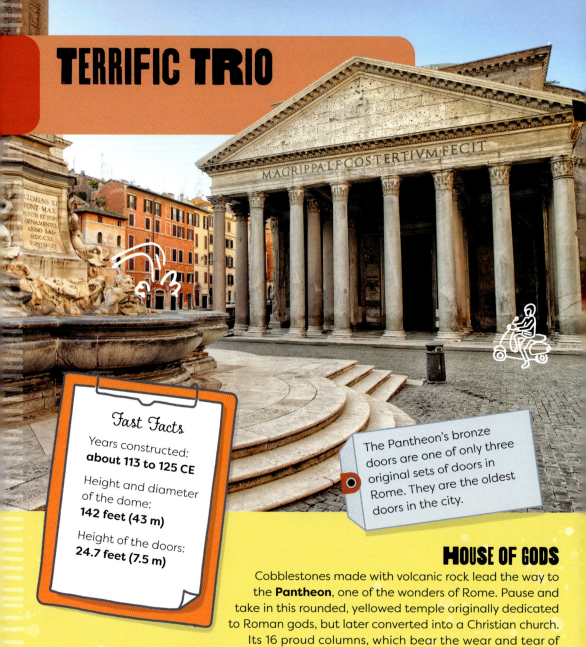

Fast Facts

Years constructed:
about 113 to 125 CE

Height and diameter of the dome:
142 feet (43 m)

Height of the doors:
24.7 feet (7.5 m)

The Pantheon's bronze doors are one of only three original sets of doors in Rome. They are the oldest doors in the city.

HOUSE OF GODS

Cobblestones made with volcanic rock lead the way to the **Pantheon**, one of the wonders of Rome. Pause and take in this rounded, yellowed temple originally dedicated to Roman gods, but later converted into a Christian church. Its 16 proud columns, which bear the wear and tear of thousands of years of history, stand tall. Enter the massive bronze doors to marvel at the crowning achievement—the dome. Through the oculus, an open "eye" in the dome's center, a beam of sunlight shines down as if from the heavens above.

72 A Kid's Guide to ROME

STEP RIGHT UP!

Named for the nearby Spanish Embassy, the **Spanish Steps** are one of Rome's most famous attractions. At dawn, dusk, or midnight, there is always a sea of people mingling on the majestic staircase. You, too, can head up the 135 steps, built more than 300 years ago. Famous writers, artists, and musicians have found inspiration here, like the English poet John Keats, who lived in an apartment at the foot of the steps and is buried in the city's Protestant Cemetery (see pages 114–115).

HEAD TO TREVI

You might hear the **Trevi Fountain** before you see it. Or is that the murmur of crowds clamoring beside its shell-shaped chariot? At Rome's most famous fountain, water almost literally comes to life. Looming tall is the star of the show, a statue of Oceanus—he represents the might of the sea. Around him are winged horses. The coins tossed into the fountain are collected twice a week, and the money is donated to charities that fund community projects, including soup kitchens and food banks.

IMAGES: Looking up the Spanish Steps (above); Trevi Fountain (left); the Pantheon (opposite).

A Hub of History 73

AN ANCIENT ROAD

HISTORIC HIGHWAY

The **Appian Way** was originally created to transport Roman troops working to maintain and expand the empire across Europe. Today, a visit to the road is a choose-your-own-adventure of ancient ruins, churches, tombs, gates, and more. Start at the park's information office to rent a bike. Ride to the tomb of Cecilia Metella—then consider a stop at the Circus Maxentius or stroll through Appia Antica Park (see pages 116–117), where the road is best preserved. Just think: you'll be following in the footsteps of emperors, pilgrims, and even saints on stones that have been fixed into place by millennia of marching feet and horse hooves. March on!

É DIVERTENTE!

In ancient Rome, the Appian Way had its own slogan: *Appia longarum, regina viarum*, meaning the Appian Way, the queen of roads!

Fast Facts

Length of tunnels: **12 miles (19 km)**

Total number of people buried: **500,000**

Number of buried popes: **16**

CALLING CALLISTO!

Built in the third century, the **Catacombs of San Callisto** was the first official Christian cemetery in Rome—and, therefore, the world. They're often called the most beautiful of the city's catacombs (see pages 56–57), and it's easy to see why: the vast underground network has four levels of graves, tunnels, family tombs, frescoes, and tiled chambers. People who traveled along the Appian Way would have walked directly above the spooky site. According to many people, one of its most remarkable treasures is the Crypt of the Popes, which houses the remains of several Catholic kings. If you dare enter, you must do so with a guided tour.

IMAGES: An ancient aqueduct (above); the gate to the Catacombs of San Callisto (left).

A Hub of History 75

THE HEART OF THE CITY

When people think about Rome, **Centro Storico** (Historic Center) is often what they imagine: a cobblestoned tangle of alleys, piazzas, ruins, and monuments, spilling over with cafés, eateries, and crowds of locals and visitors alike. The streets are open-air museums of Baroque and Renaissance art history.

You might be familiar with some of its famous sites, like the Pantheon (see page 72) and Piazza Navona (see pages 36–37). But take some time to explore its many small *chiese* (churches) and their art collections, too.

Centro Storico is the best place to fully experience Rome's many layers. Here, among priceless pieces of history, you'll also see the vibrant, beating heart of the city—its people. Weave through the *mercati rionali* (local markets), and shop with everyday Romans. Like Rome throughout the ages, the city is still changing with the times.

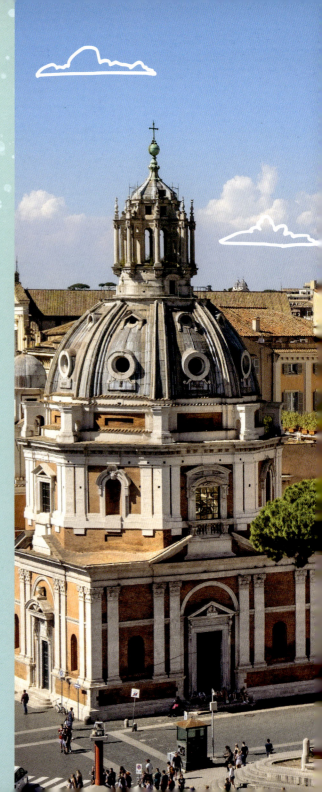

IMAGE: A view of Centro Storico.

Il Vittoriano, a monument in Centro Storico, is nicknamed "the typewriter" for its unusual shape.

Shrine Scavenger Hunt
See if you can spot an *edicola sacra* hiding in plain sight on the street. Like a treasured locket, these "corner shrines" hold a painting, mosaic, or tiny sculpture—and they're everywhere.

VISIT THE VATICAN

WORLD'S SMALLEST COUNTRY

Grab your passport and visit the smallest independent nation in the world! Nestled in the heart of old Rome, **Vatican City** is just 0.17 square mile (0.44 sq km). It's also the seat, or official center, of the Roman Catholic Church. The body of government is called the Holy See, and the pope is both the head of the church and the sovereign of the Holy See. Talk about responsibility! Travelers can tour the country's museums and basilica. More daring visitors can also book a tour to the necropolis, or cemetery. The Vatican Gardens, which cover about half of the country, are dotted with fountains, hedges, and trickling ponds. There is even a cactus garden!

Fast Facts

Population: **roughly 1,000 people, including the pope**

Number of Swiss Guards protecting the pope: **135**

Number of annual visitors: **5 million**

The news of a new pope is broadcast via smoke signal from the Sistine Chapel! A special chimney lets the cardinals release their results: white smoke means a pope has been chosen; black smoke means no one received the majority vote.

MIGHTY MUSEUMS

Pope Julius II established the **Vatican Museums** in the 16th century. Today, the museums display some 20,000 works from several thousand years of human history. You'll also see the Sistine Chapel (see page 93), and the Raphael Rooms, including Renaissance-era paintings by iconic artists like Caravaggio and Leonardo da Vinci. You might have the most fun stumbling upon some of the lesser-known galleries, like the Gallery of Maps or the Hall of Animals. In all, there are 54 galleries and 1,400 rooms!

IMAGES: A view of St. Peter's Basilica (above); the Nile statue inside the Vatican Museums (left).

THE MAIN EVENT

The Colosseum has survived earthquakes, fires—and stone robbers.

Fast Facts

Size: about 600 feet (180 m) long, 500 feet (150 m) wide, and 12 stories tall—big enough to fit a football field

Years built: **constructed between 72 CE and 80 CE**

ENTER THE COLOSSEUM

No monument holds a torch to the **Colosseum**. At nearly 2,000 years old, it remains the largest amphitheater ever built. The stands could fit some 60,000 Romans! This feat of architecture and engineering offers more than stunning visuals. A tour will unlock secrets of the ruins, like how a retractable roof (*velarium*) once provided shade during sweltering summers. Exploring the ancient arena by moonlight makes nighttime visits especially epic!

80 A Kid's Guide to ROME

MAN VS. BEAST

Who dares enter the arena? Some gladiators were trained professionals seeking fortune or glory in one-on-one combat. Others were forced to fight as a form of cruel criminal punishment or enslavement. One harsh punishment was *damnatio ad bestias*—death by beasts, which were often lions imported from northern Africa. The fights were often harsh and gory.

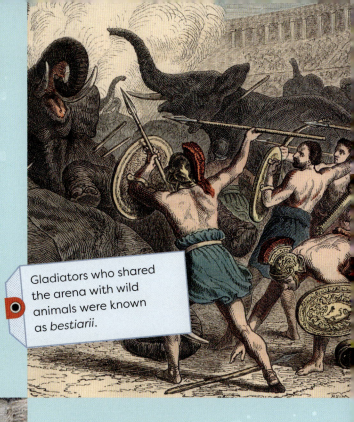

Gladiators who shared the arena with wild animals were known as *bestiarii*.

BACKSTAGE PASS

The Colosseum's *hypogeum* was a system of underground tunnels. In these long, shadowy passageways, fearsome animals snarled in cages, and gladiators readied their spears, daggers, and tridents. Stagehands used elevators and trapdoors to transport both man and beast to the arena above in truly spectacular fashion. Today, you can experience this "backstage" like a VIP. Exploring the now uncovered labyrinth paints a picture of the Colosseum as it was: a bustling hive of activity.

IMAGES: An engraving of an ancient Colosseum event (above); the *hypogeum* within the Colosseum (left); the Colosseum (opposite).

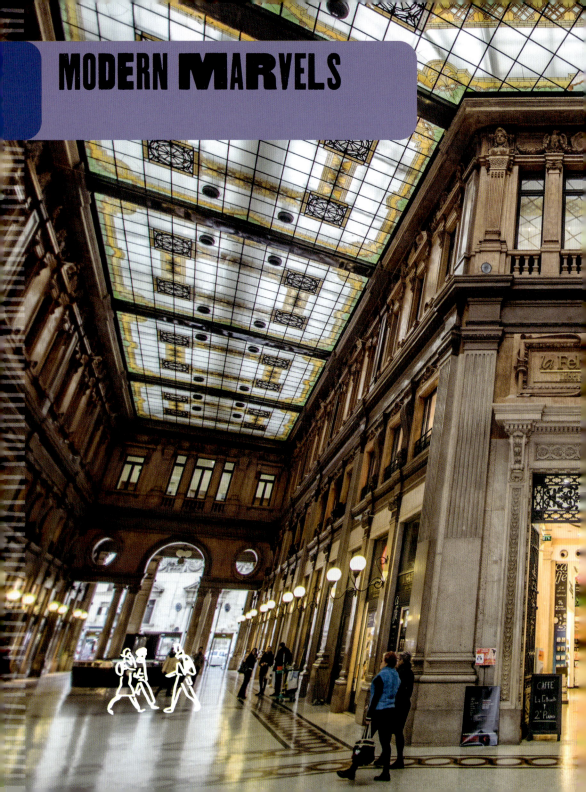

MODERN MARVELS

IMAGE: The interior of the Galleria Alberto Sordi.

OF CORSO!

If you could peek in on **Via del Corso** during different points in time, you might see religious pilgrims on their way to the Vatican or wild crowds of people celebrating Carnival. But Romans of every period have mingled and shopped on this historic street.

Start your trek at Piazza del Popolo (see pages 36–37) and wander the street's fashionable shops before ending at **Piazza Venezia**. Along the way, make sure to pause at **Galleria Alberto Sordi** and admire the gallery's stained-glass ceilings, globe lamps, and totally cool tile floors.

For a behind-the-scenes view of the arts, take a walking tour with the Botteghiamo Project, a group promoting traditional artwork. Enter a secret world of workshops, where traditional goldsmiths, mosaicists, dollmakers, ceramists, violinmakers, and many more still practice their crafts. Ask to see the group's hand-illustrated map of the city's most fascinating and historic workshops.

On Via Tiburtina, chocolatiers at SAID 1923, a chocolate factory and café, have been running a chocolate "laboratory" for three generations.

IMAGE: Piazza Venezia and the Altare della Patria monument at Christmastime.

84   A Kid's Guide to ROME

ON YOUR MARKS...
Via del Corso gets its name from the *corsa dei barberi*, an annual horse race held during Carnival. There were no riders—horses would be gathered next to the obelisk in Piazza del Popolo and "launched" toward Piazza Venezia. It was more like a horse stampede!

FAR-OUT FOUNTAINS

AWESOME AQUEDUCTS

Aqueducts once kept the Roman Empire's growing population hydrated and bathed. These amazing architectural wonders carried fresh spring water into the city from up to 57 miles (92 km) away using a simple tool: gravity. Today, some are still in use, like the **Aqua Virgo**, which feeds the Trevi Fountain (see page 73). The age-old design needs no improvement!

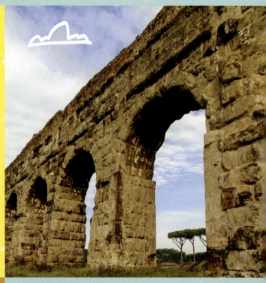

NOSEDIVE INTO NASONI

While you can find drinking water shooting from the city's impressive marble fountain monuments—yes, you can drink from those!—you'll also find smaller stone *nasoni* scattered along city streets. Nasoni, or "big noses," refers to the shape of their signature metal spouts. These fountains are never turned off, so the pipes' constant flow keeps the water fresh. Drink up!

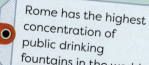

Rome has the highest concentration of public drinking fountains in the world.

86 A Kid's Guide to ROME

CITY OF WATER

Get your water shoes on and tour the **Vicus Caprarius!** This historic housing complex was discovered near the Trevi Fountain—completely underground. The subterranean site is a winding maze of brick walls, arches, and hallways where residents once lived out their daily lives. The Aqua Virgo aqueduct drips water into the honeycomb of buildings on its way to feed the fountain.

Fast Facts

Vicus Caprarius depth underground: **around 30 feet (9 m)**

Number of ancient coins discovered on-site: **800**

A SINKING SHIP?

Built in 1629, **Barcaccia Fountain** in Piazza di Spagna tells the story of a small boat that was carried into the piazza by a Tiber River flood. When the waters receded, the boat was left stranded on the city streets. Oops! While we can't be sure the tale is totally true, the artist Pietro Bernini thought it was entertaining enough to immortalize in marble. Admire the half-submerged ship and two sun-shaped faces as they spit water right back into the unlucky boat.

IMAGES: Vicus Caprarius (above); the Barcaccia Fountain (right); the Aqua Appia aqueduct (opposite top); a young girl drinking from a nasone (opposite bottom).

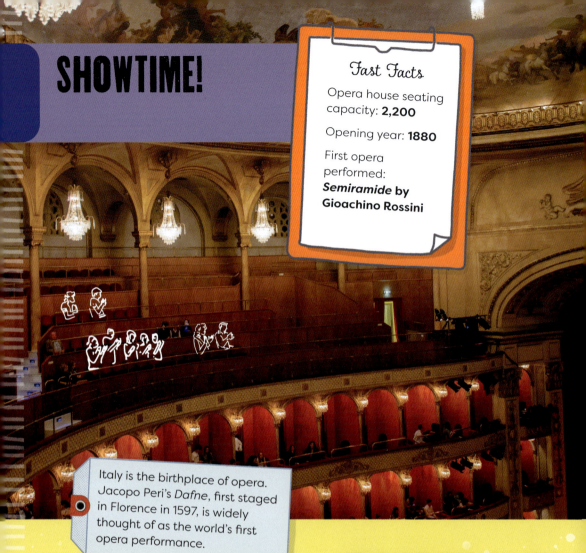

SHOWTIME!

Fast Facts

Opera house seating capacity: **2,200**

Opening year: **1880**

First opera performed: ***Semiramide*** **by Gioachino Rossini**

Italy is the birthplace of opera. Jacopo Peri's *Dafne*, first staged in Florence in 1597, is widely thought of as the world's first opera performance.

GRAB YOUR OPERA GLASSES

Experience Italian opera at its finest with a ticket to **Teatro dell'Opera**, Rome's primary opera house. The theater is not only gorgeous, with ceiling paintings and ornate railings, but it's also an acoustic powerhouse. The carefully designed architecture makes the music sound better than any high-tech electronic speaker could. Don't miss the classic children's shows! Most operas have subtitles, but even if you can't understand the words, there's costumes, sets, and so much more to keep you entertained!

IMAGES: Inside the Teatro dell'Opera (above); two people training at Gladiator School (opposite top); outside Cinema dei Piccoli (opposite bottom).

88   A Kid's Guide to ROME

GO GLADIATOR

Leave your backpack at home and enroll in **Gladiator School**! Here, you can practice the techniques of ancient Roman gladiators, plus learn a little bit about gladiator history. The average lesson includes a two-hour combat training session and (fake) weapons. You can even rent gladiator clothes! Then head to the gladiator-inspired museum. As a bonus, you and your family can enjoy a reenactment of a gladiator fight, ancient dance, or Roman legion (army) maneuvers.

Piccoli means "little ones" in Italian.

TINY THEATER

First opened in 1934, the **Cinema dei Piccoli** holds the record for smallest cinema building in the world. The tiny theater packs a huge punch: in addition to showing cartoons in many languages, fairy tales, popular kids movies, and classic animated features, the miniature movie house has hands-on activities that pair with movies. Here, you can take a workshop in toymaking or animation. Most magical of all, you'll find this quaint green cottage tucked inside the lush gardens of the Villa Borghese (see page 108).

Modern Marvels 89

FEAST YOUR EYES

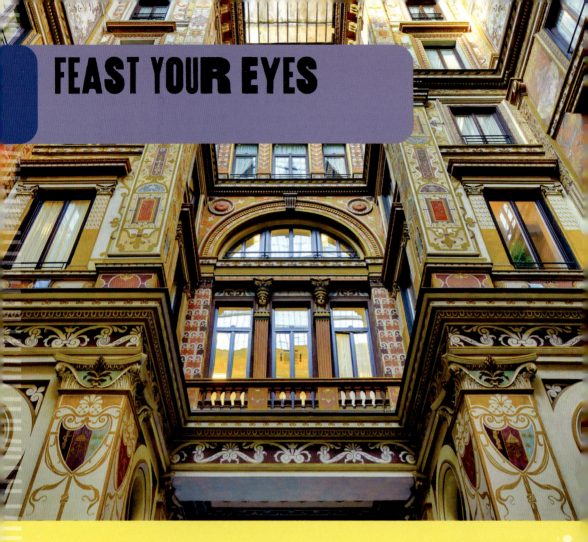

NOUVEAU ART

Just a few steps away from Via del Corso (see pages 84–85) is the **Galleria Sciarra**, a grand courtyard designed and decorated in the art nouveau style. What on *earth* is that? Earth is right—art nouveau is inspired by flowers, plants, and natural forms like curves. Compared to older artistic styles, like the Baroque art that defines the city's sculptures and fountains, art nouveau is blooming with color. The galleria takes a turn from Rome's many marble monuments. Every inch of the courtyard's colorful frescoes and floral patterns offers new details to enjoy.

IMAGES: The decoration of Galleria Sciarra (above); Casina delle Civette (opposite top); the San Carlino Puppet Theater (opposite bottom).

THE OWLS' HOUSE

Among Rome's many wonders is the **Casina delle Civette** (House of Owls). Nestled in Villa Torlonia, the secluded building seems like it belongs to another world. That's what made it the perfect hideout for the prince who lived here when he needed a break from his duties. Inside, you'll feel as though you were dropped right into your own fairy tale. Surround yourself with sculpted birds, painted woodland scenes, and whimsical stained-glass windows that depict lots of animals like swans, horses—and, yes, owls!

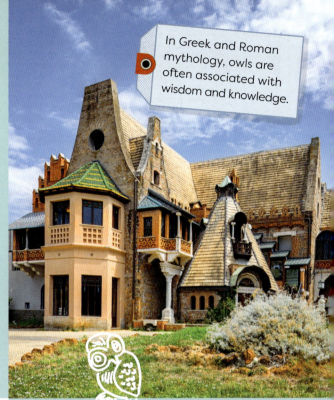

In Greek and Roman mythology, owls are often associated with wisdom and knowledge.

MERRY MARIONETTES

After catching a movie in the Cinema dei Piccoli, stroll down the Viale dei Bambini to the **San Carlino Puppet Theater**. Bright costumes, handmade puppets, and interactive storytelling make these traditional shows one of Rome's best activities. The puppet performances are a hilarious way to spend an afternoon. Shows are in Italian, but you won't need to know the language to understand the fun (and funny) storytelling!

The now famous story of the mischievous puppet Pinocchio was written by an Italian author in the 19th century.

Modern Marvels 91

UNRIVALED ARTWORK

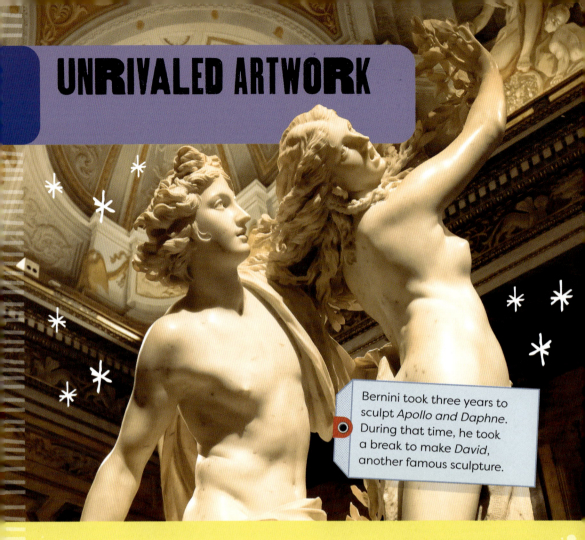

Bernini took three years to sculpt *Apollo and Daphne*. During that time, he took a break to make *David*, another famous sculpture.

MARBLE MARVEL

One of the world's most famous statues can be found in Rome. **Apollo and Daphne** by Gian Lorenzo Bernini depicts the god Apollo as he chases Daphne, a nymph. But Daphne will not be caught—see how her hands turn into leafy branches? The scene looks frozen in place, as if the figures are going to come to life at any moment to finish the chase, and Daphne will complete her transformation into a tree. Visit the statue in the Galleria Borghese (see page 52) to marvel at Bernini's magical ability to turn hard stone into what looks like flexible, soft skin.

IMAGES: Apollo and Daphne by Gian Lorenzo Bernini (above); a section of The School of Athens by Raphael (opposite top); the ceiling of the Sistine Chapel (opposite bottom).

RAPHAEL'S ROOMS

Even among the Vatican Museums' (see pages 78–79) mind-bending collection of artwork, Renaissance artist Raphael's frescoes stand out. There are four Raphael Rooms inside. Each contains spectacular painted scenes on all the walls (and sometimes on the ceiling, too). **The School of Athens** gets the A+. This fresco is an imaginary scene depicting a who's who of ancient Greek philosophers, scientists, and writers. Raphael created the genius works after being commissioned by the pope to decorate. That's some *really* fancy wallpaper.

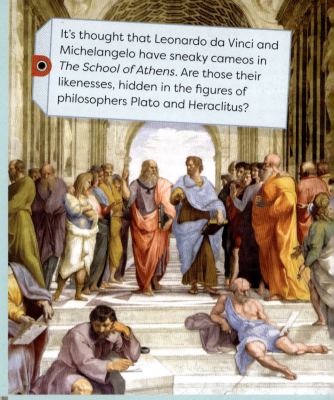

It's thought that Leonardo da Vinci and Michelangelo have sneaky cameos in *The School of Athens*. Are those their likenesses, hidden in the figures of philosophers Plato and Heraclitus?

MICHELANGELO'S MASTERPIECE

Look up! Painted by Michelangelo more than 500 years ago, the magnificent ceiling of the **Sistine Chapel** tells the story of the Book of Genesis, the first book of the Old Testament of the Christian Bible. The second of nine scenes is *The Creation of Adam*, one of the most well-known images in art history, which depicts the Hand of God giving life to Adam. The effect of looking up at the kaleidoscopic panels gives visitors the feeling of being inside the painting. At first, the bold paints, twisting figures, and clashing angels seem chaotic—but once your eyes adjust, you will see the story told in perfectly planned images.

Modern Marvels 93

THE WILD SIDE

IMAGE: *A fox nestling in the grass.*

WONDERFUL WOLVES

The story of Rome begins with a wolf. According to legend, it was a female wolf who nursed Rome's founders, Remus and Romulus (see page 49), back to health after they were abandoned to die in the Tiber River. This she-wolf has been depicted endlessly in Roman art, including statues, frescoes, altars, mosaics, and even on coins. (See how many you can spot!)

Real wolves—a type of gray wolf—once roamed the country. But they were hunted nearly to extinction in the 19th and 20th centuries. Are wolves in Rome only a thing of history?

Hopefully not. Just a few years ago, a family of wild wolves was spotted by trail cameras in **Castel di Guido Reserve**, a dense thicket of nature near the airport. Regardless of how rare the wolf has become, the four-legged beast remains Rome's longest-lasting and fiercest symbol.

IMAGE: Two wolves in the Italian countryside.

Fast Facts

Common name:
Italian wolf or Apennine wolf

Average weight:
60 to 90 pounds (27 to 41 kg)

Average height:
26 to 32 inches (66 to 81 cm)

Throughout Italy, there are an estimated 3,000 wolves roaming in the wild.

ANIMALS IN ART
Rome is full of animal art. Can you find the Egyptian lions in Michelangelo's Piazza del Campidoglio? Gian Lorenzo Bernini's elephant in Piazza della Minerva? Or Turtle Fountain in Piazza Mattei? The sculpted dragons and water horses in Villa Borghese? The Fountain of the Bees? It's a zoo out there!

CALLING ALL CATS

THE PU**RR**-FECT PLACE

Cats are an important part of the city's past. They were considered sacred to Diana, the Roman goddess of wild animals and the hunt. Plus, they were great at catching pests! This appreciation for felines continues today: in modern Rome, cats are protected by law and cannot be harmed or even relocated. The cat-loving culture has led to the formation of Rome's famous cat colonies, or large communities of feral cats. Most famous is the **Torre Argentina Cat Sanctuary**, where more than 100 felines can be spotted lounging on the temple ruins. Another notable open-air shelter is located on the grounds of the **Pyramid of Caius Cestius** and the adjacent cemetery.

BLESS THESE CATS

St. Anthony is the patron saint of animals. Every year on the Feast of St. Anthony, pet owners bring their fur babies to Chiesa di Sant'Eusebio and farmers bring their livestock to St. Peter's Square to be blessed.

KITTY CARE

All those cats need someone to take care of them—enter *le gattare*, Rome's self-appointed cat caretakers. As the first "official" cat colony grew when the ruins of Torre Argentina were uncovered nearly a century ago, a group of women began to feed their feline friends leftover meat and fish. Today, le gattare have grown into a group of organized volunteers who feed and vaccinate the cats, as well as collaborate with veterinarians to oversee spaying and neutering. They will even adopt out a select few to lucky families.

IMAGES: An orange tabby at the Torre Argentina Cat Sanctuary (above); a care station at the sanctuary (left).

The Wild Side 99

AMAZING ANIMALS

IT'S A ZOO!

Rome's **Bioparco**, one of Europe's oldest zoos, was built in the beautiful Villa Borghese gardens (see page 108) more than 100 years ago. Today, it's a thriving center for endangered animal conservation. Here, you'll find a menagerie of feathered, clawed, and furry creatures. Behind the scenes, zoologists are studying the eating habits of their African penguin colony and the behaviors of the resident Himalayan tahrs (relatives of goats and sheep). The zoo regularly hosts activities, which sometimes involve up-close animal encounters!

Fast Facts

Year founded: **1932**

Number of specimens: **5 million**

Largest specimen: **a 52-foot-long (16 m) whale skeleton**

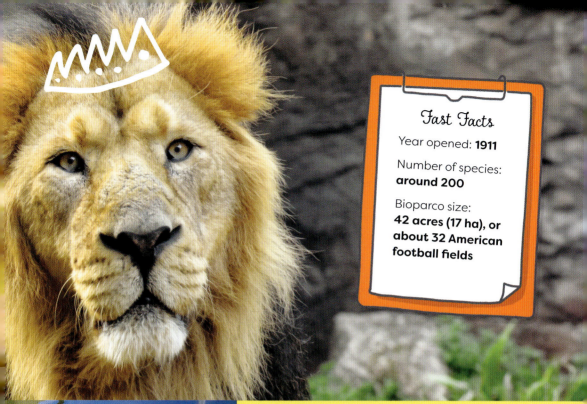

Fast Facts

Year opened: **1911**

Number of species: **around 200**

Bioparco size: **42 acres (17 ha), or about 32 American football fields**

AN ABUNDANCE OF OLOGIES

Next to the Bioparco is the **Museo Civico di Zoologia**—Rome's natural history museum. You won't find any living animals here, but you will discover a seemingly never-ending maze of animal taxidermy and well-preserved specimens, from tiny invertebrates to a massive minke whale skeleton. If you're interested in ichthyology, the study of fish, check out the museum's collection of spooky-looking sea lampreys from the Tiber River. The herpetological (reptile) collections include giant Nile crocodile skulls and rare Japanese salamanders preserved in liquid!

IMAGES: A lion at Bioparco (above); displays at the Museo Civico di Zoologia (left).

The Wild Side

ON THE STREETS OF GRROME

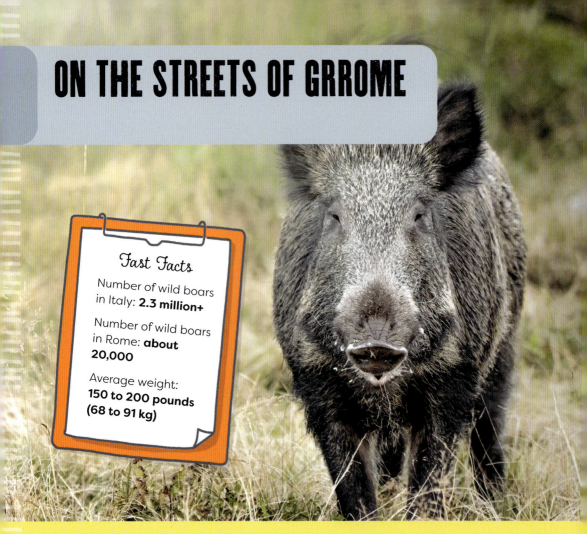

Fast Facts

Number of wild boars in Italy: **2.3 million+**

Number of wild boars in Rome: **about 20,000**

Average weight: **150 to 200 pounds (68 to 91 kg)**

MIND THE BOARS

Rome has been sacked, or defeated and looted, many times in its long history. From barbarian vandals to imperial armies, many have raided the city for its treasures. The tradition of looting Rome continues today—except now the invading brutes are wild boars! The wild boar population has exploded across Italy in recent years due to a lack of natural predators. These large, hairy, and hoofed cinghiali regularly dive through trash cans and disrupt relaxing outdoor picnics. Take the cinghiali seriously and do not approach: wild boars can be dangerous!

SEEING RED (FOXES)

Like in the rest of Europe, foxes have made themselves at home in the Eternal City. Cities provide these sleek canines plenty of opportunities to scavenge from dumpsters, trash cans, and even restaurant trash. Red foxes are frequent visitors to the city's many parks. **Villa Pamphili** has its own locally famous fox, Olimpia, named after the 17th-century princess whose family once owned the villa. She even has a boyfriend, Giulio!

NOT A BEAVER!

Rome's most adorable wildlife citizen might just be the nutria. Though Romans sometimes use the term *castorino* (little beaver), the nutria is not a true beaver. You can tell the difference by observing the nutria's long, round tail, which is different from a beaver's distinct flat tail. Keep an eye on the Tiber River, where these rodents have been known to swim and gather on the shore. Nutria also have webbed feet, thick fur, and large chompers. Do not pet them!

IMAGES: A Roman fox (above); a nutria taking a dip (left); a wild boar (opposite).

The Wild Side 103

TAKING FLIGHT

GREAT GULLS

Today, herring gulls seem to have control of Rome's streets, dive-bombing for discarded food scraps, terrorizing the pigeon population, and squatting on the heads of stately statues. Why are there so many? Lots of people think the white-and-gray-winged birds descended on Rome when a large landfill on the city's outskirts—the gulls preferred home—was permanently closed.

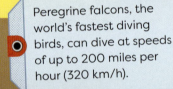

Peregrine falcons, the world's fastest diving birds, can dive at speeds of up to 200 miles per hour (320 km/h).

PEREGRINE COMEBACK

The peregrine falcon almost went extinct in Italy in the 1970s, but the majestic bird has been making a comeback in recent decades. Conservation workers have even placed well-hidden artificial nests on tall structures, such as telephone poles and water towers, to help the birds thrive. Scientists monitor some avian couples using live webcams. Anyone can view the live streams and observe these growing families from a safe distance!

A PARAKEET FLEET

No, you haven't been transported to the jungle—you just ran into some of Rome's famous parakeets! These tropical South American birds are descended from escaped or released exotic pets. Though they are not native to Italy, they have thrived in the warm, moist Mediterranean climate. Parakeets can be found soaring through Centro Storico, swooping over Palatine Hill, or settling down on the branches of Rome's diverse array of pine trees.

> There are two parakeet species found in Rome: monk parakeets and rose-ringed parakeets.

SWARM OF STARLINGS

Every winter, millions of starlings migrate to Rome in search of warm weather. They gather at dusk in a synchronized aerial dance called a murmuration, covering the twilight sky like an undulating black cloud. The display over the skyline is beautiful—but do you have any idea how much a million birds can poop? Enough that people carry umbrellas for protection! City officials have tried to disperse the birds, but these starlings are stubborn.

IMAGES: A parakeet snacking on fruit (above); a murmuration of starlings at sunset (right); a gull perching on a rooftop (opposite top); a peregrine falcon (opposite bottom).

GOING GREEN

IMAGE: The Orange Garden.

GARDEN DELIGHTS

The Villa Borghese park has a replica of England's Globe Theatre, where Shakespeare staged his plays.

A NOBLE GARDEN

On the slopes of Pincian Hill is an oasis of art, flowing fountains, and gorgeous green spaces. At nearly 200 acres (81 ha), **Villa Borghese** is not the largest landscaped park in Rome—Villa Doria Pamphilj and Villa Ada are bigger—but its central, large open spaces are extremely popular and fun to explore! Those with a need for speed can rent a bike or even a quadricycle. If your legs get tired, hop on the park's miniature train for a relaxing ride.

ESCAPE TO THE LAKE

The human-made **Giardino del Lago** provides a scenic spot to refresh your senses, sit back, and enjoy nature. Here, you can bird-watch: see if you can find the villa's kingfishers, warblers, and parakeets on your visit. Get on the move with a walk along the **Viale del Lago** trail or rent a rowboat and hit the water. Keep an eye out for the **Temple of Aesculapius**, located on a little island in the lake. It's home to a statue of Aesculapius, the god of medicine.

LITTLE HOUSE, BIG FUN

Almost smack in the center of Villa Borghese is **Casina di Raffaello**, an indoor play center. The *casina*, or "little house," has activities, games, toys, a reading room, and a bookshop. When you're done having fun inside, enjoy the outdoor space set among the lush greenery of the villa. Then walk in the direction of Piazza del Popolo (see pages 36–37) along the Viale dei Bambini, where you can check the time at an unusual 19th-century water clock!

IMAGES: Boating on Giardino del Lago (above); the Villa Borghese water clock (left); fountains in Villa Borghese Park (opposite).

Going Green 109

WHAT'S GROWING ON?

Rome's farmers markets, known as *mercati rionali*, offer up loads of local goods. Often found in the centers of Rome's *rioni*, they're hubs for social activities—and, of course, some great shopping!

The weekend farmers market at Circo Massimo (see pages 42–43) is full of fun foods to try. The 100-year-old **Testaccio Market** is home to 100 stalls operating inside the glass-roofed building. This large market is a favorite among locals.

In Trastevere, **San Cosimato** has a used books stall, wandering dogs who seek out the market's dog food, and a playground in the piazza! Another must-see market, just around the corner from the Vatican, is **Mercato Trionfale**, considered the first Roman market. It's also one of the largest in Europe! You can find just about anything among the 270 indoor stalls. Long ago, this area was a transit area for hunters or travelers to stop for a bite to eat or for people to rest and feed their horses. Today, it's an exciting place to explore and shop.

IMAGE: Campo de' Fiori market.

AHEAD OF HIS TIME

At Campo de' Fiori, find the statue of Giordano Bruno—an outspoken monk who, among other things, believed that Earth revolved around the sun long before the science was accepted. He was killed for his heresy (defiance of the church) in this square. Today, he is a symbol of defiance—that's why he's facing the direction of the Vatican. Campo de' Fiori is still a gathering place for protests.

TOUR THE TIBER!

EXPLORE OSTIA

Attention, swimmers! The beachfront town of **Ostia** is only about a one-hour train ride away from Centro Storico. Enjoy an afternoon of relaxation and swimming in the shallow waters, then stroll the *Lungomare* (promenade) to browse the shops. Along the coast, sand dunes have protected buildings from erosion, preserving important pieces of history for centuries to come. Right next to the mouth of the Tiber River, this seaside oasis has beaches *and* forests. Nearby is Ostia Antica. This well-preserved harbor city has an ancient cemetery and restaurant to explore!

Fast Facts

Length of Tiber River: **252 miles (405 km)**

River's source: **Mount Fumaiolo**

River's mouth: **Tyrrhenian Sea**

H2O HIGHWAY

As Rome's original drinking source and waterway for trade, the mighty Tiber River is one of the city's greatest treasures. Whether you're on foot or on a bike, you can use the path of the *Lungotevere*, the river waterfront. Stop by **Tor di Quinto Park** to look for waterbirds. For a more adrenaline-pumping experience, take a kayak or canoe ride to cross underneath bridges like Ponte Cestio, Ponte Fabricio, and the age-old Ponte Rotto. You'll be paddling the same routes as the ancient merchants who carried the travertine marble for city monuments and wheat to feed Rome's people.

IMAGES: The beach in Ostia (above); the Tiber River and the Lungotevere path (left).

Going Green 113

PEACEFUL RETREATS

A PLACE TO REST

The **Protestant Cemetery** is one of Europe's oldest burial grounds still in use. The first grave was placed here in 1738! It is meant for non-Catholics and non-Romans. Here, you'll find the graves of people who fell in love with Rome, including Romantic poets John Keats and Percy Bysshe Shelley, and many more notable people. Among the cemetery's living visitors are a familiar Roman sight: cats! This is the site of one of Rome's many cat colonies (see pages 98–99).

Orto Botanico's collection includes carnivorous plants, such as the Venus flytrap.

PAST THE PYRAMID

The cemetery is tucked behind the Pyramid of Caius Cestius, the only pyramid in Europe. Little is known about Gaius Cestius, who had this tomb built, but the well-preserved structure is even older than the Colosseum!

BOUNTIFUL BLOOMS

Rome's **Orto Botanico**, or Botanical Garden, is the perfect place to take a break from the city's hustle and bustle. The gardens have been around since 1545—almost 500 years! Here, you're greeted with a symphony of birdsong and a green sanctuary of 6,000 plants from all over the world. The Japanese Garden bursts with magnolias, cherry blossoms, waterfalls, and ponds. In the Herb Garden, there are medicinal plants that have been used by Romans for thousands of years. The Rose Garden is in full bloom in May, when about 60 different species come to life!

IMAGES: A cat sitting atop a headstone in the Protestant Cemetery (above); Orto Botanico in Trastevere (left).

ON THE OUTSKIRTS

GROW WILD

The colossal **Appia Antica Park** holds a section of the Appian Way (see pages 74-75), the Eternal City's most famous road. But it's also a nature park with a treasure trove of wonders! Its green corridor is a haven for nesting birds, wandering foxes, and hopping amphibians. Underneath the corridor is a fascinating geology: the park sits on hardened lava flows and deposits from the volcanic Alban Hills. Appia Antica is among the largest parks in all of Europe—and unlike Rome's many carefully cultivated villas, it has been left to grow wild.

Fast Facts

Length of Aqua Marcia: **56.5 miles (91 km)**

Aqua Marcia's carrying capacity: **50 million gallons (189 million L) daily**

Appia Antica Park is home to at least one active farm. Venture to the overgrown Caffarella Valley to spot horses, flocks of sheep—and maybe even a llama!

AWESOME ARCHES

Aqueduct Park, which is part of the Appia Antica network, boasts 6 of the 11 original aqueducts that carried water into ancient Rome. These six—Anio Vetus, Aqua Tepula, Aqua Marcia, Aqua Claudio, Aqua Julia, and Anio Novus—have stood here for thousands of years. (Well, Anio Vetus is actually underground.) In the shadows of these magnificent arches, you can enjoy a picnic or rent a bicycle to explore the park's many pine tree-lined paths. Stop by at sunset to see the arches appear to glow!

IMAGES: Peering down the Via Appia Antica (above); morning at Aqueduct Park (left).

Going Green

SECRETS OF THE CITY

IMAGE: Gian Lorenzo Bernini's colonnades at St. Peter's Square.

ITALIAN ILLUSIONS

DON'T BLINK
Artist Andrea Pozzo used a painterly trick called trompe l'oeil—meaning "to deceive the eye"—to build a dome at the Jesuit **Church of St. Ignazio**. In reality, though, the dome was just a flat painting! People were so pleased that he did it again to create a new scene of the heavens. Look up to feel as though you're being pulled into the sky by cherubs. Markers on the church floor tell you where to stand for the best angle.

GET SOME PERSPECTIVE
Venture to the courtyard of **Palazzo Spada** to be duped by architect Francesco Borromini. You might think you see a super-long hallway flanked by columns leading to a giant statue of the Roman mythological god Mars. But it seems impossibly far away! Therein lies Borromini's deceit—the hall is just 26 feet (8 m) long, and the statue is only 24 inches (60 cm) tall! Using mathematics, he created a perspective gallery that has been fooling people for hundreds of years.

A DISAPPEARING ACT

Hop over to **St. Peter's Square** in Vatican City to find the two striking semicircular colonnades. From most vantage points, you'll see that each has four rows of columns. Then, go to the square center and find the sneakily subtle marble disks sunken into the ground. One is inscribed: *centro del colonnato* (center of the colonnade). Look up from that exact spot, and ta-da! Three rows of columns will have disappeared, leaving only one. Gian Lorenzo Bernini is responsible for this magic act.

MAKE SOME MAGIC

If you want to go from tricked to trickster, head to the **Museum of Illusions**, just a short walk from the Colosseum. Here, you can learn the science and math behind great illusions and even test some out yourself. Dizzying turntables and mind-bending holograms are just the beginning. Are you daring enough to enter the Vortex Tunnel or the Upside Down Room? Are you ready to defy gravity in the Infinity Room? Just remember—nothing is as it seems.

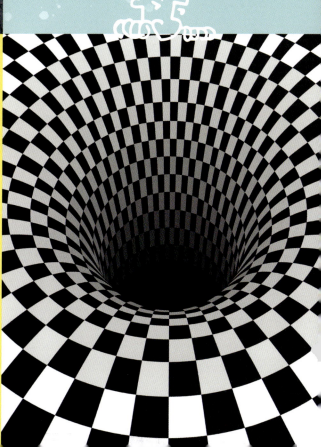

IMAGES: A view of Bernini's colonnades (above); a common optical illusion (right); the interior of the Church of St. Ignazio (opposite top); Borromini's forced perspective gallery in Palazzo Spada (opposite bottom).

MONSTERS, MYTHS, AND PORTALS

LIFE'S A FAIRY TALE

The whimsical neighborhood of **Quartiere Coppedè** mixes modern architecture styles with classical touches to create a wacky style all its own. Grand buildings like Palazzina del Ragno (Spider Palace) and Villino delle Fate (Fairy House), along with decorations showcasing mythical creatures, will make you think you've fallen headfirst into a storybook. Outside, toss a coin into the Fountain of Frogs. Here, it feels like anything you can dream up is possible.

HOUSE OF MONSTERS

Watch out or you will be eaten by a monster! The facade, or exterior, of **Zuccari Palace** is sculpted with giant monster faces opening their mouths (or chomping down!) to reveal the building's doors and windows. This royal monstrosity was designed in the 16th century as a studio for the architect and his children. Compared to Rome's other palazzi, the "Monster House" is a *scream*.

> One of Poland's queens once resided in Zuccari Palace.

122 A Kid's Guide to ROME

KNOCK, KNOCK

Legend says that the nobleman who built **Porta Alchemica** met an alchemist one night. The alchemist said he could teach the man how to turn metals into gold—but then the alchemist vanished, leaving only poorly scrawled instructions behind. The nobleman carved the strange "recipe" on his villa doors hoping that someone else would decipher it. To try to find this mysterious door and decode the script, look for the stout Egyptian-inspired statues that stand guard. Knock if you dare!

> An alchemist transforms natural materials, usually metals, into other substances. Some alchemists were early chemists.

FIBBERS, BEWARE

The Bocca della Verità, or Mouth of Truth, is a 2,800-pound (1,270-kg) marble mask on display in the entrance of **Basilica of St. Mary in Cosmedin**. It is said to bite the hands off liars! People have been sticking their hands into the mouth for at least several hundred years to prove their honesty. Some historians believe it is a depiction of the Greek sea titan Oceanus—and that it might have been first used as a sewer drain!

IMAGES: The Porta Alchemica (above); the Mouth of Truth (right); Quartiere Coppedè (opposite top); the monstrous entrance to Zuccari Palace (opposite bottom).

RELICS OF ROME

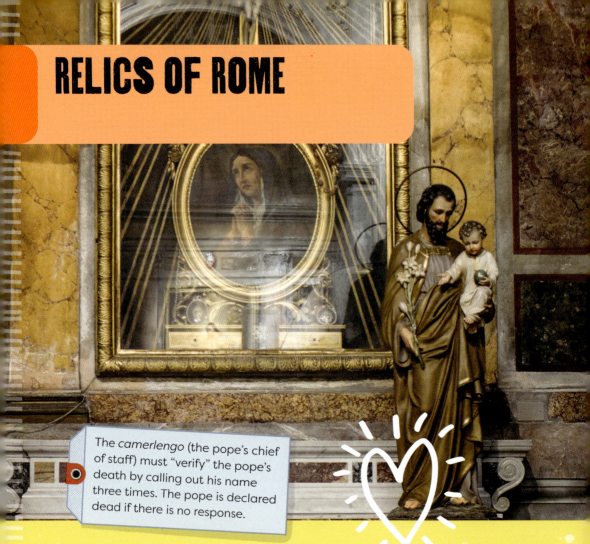

The *camerlengo* (the pope's chief of staff) must "verify" the pope's death by calling out his name three times. The pope is declared dead if there is no response.

TAKE HEART

A religious relic is an object of worship, usually an artifact—or, in some cases, a body part. If that doesn't make your stomach flip, visit the **Santi Vincenzo e Anastasio** church near the Trevi Fountain, where 22 embalmed papal hearts are stored and displayed in jars. Why are so many popes missing their hearts? A custom called *praecordia* dictated that organs should be removed from a corpse to prevent decay while the funeral was being planned. According to strict papal rules, a funeral must occur four to six days after a pope's death.

IMAGES: The interior of Santi Vincenzo e Anastasio (above); the remains of Anna Maria Taigi inside Basilica of San Crisogono (opposite top); the Lateran Basilica (opposite bottom).

THE WAX WOMAN

Popes aren't the only ones made into relics. Anna Maria Taigi, a 19th-century Roman, was thought to possess holy gifts, including visions of the past, present, and future. After her death in 1837, religious pilgrims traveled to her resting place to receive blessings, and her popularity rose. When she finally began to decompose, her hands and face were covered in wax replicas of her image. Today, her remains are still on display in a glass coffin at the **Basilica of San Crisogono**.

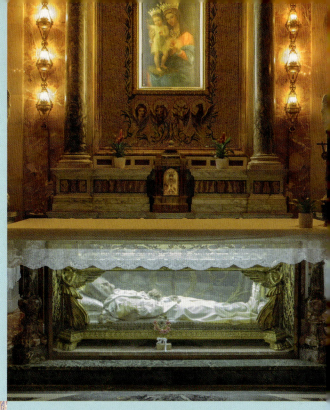

LOOKING FOR SIGNS

The tradition of divining—attempting to interpret the future through signs—is alive and well at the **Lateran Basilica**. Here, practically hidden among statues of the apostles and papal tombs, is a cenotaph—or monument to someone buried elsewhere—that "sweats" whenever a pope is about to die. How does a monument sweat? No one really knows, but believers in the legend say that the stone weeps. The cenotaph in question was built to honor the death of Pope Sylvester II.

According to one urban legend, Pope Sylvester II's skeleton will rattle when a pope is close to death.

Secrets of the City 125

ONE-OF-A-KIND SIGHTS

COVER YOUR EARS!

Every day, a blank cannon round is fired from **Janiculum Hill**. Pope Pius IX started the tradition in 1847 to synchronize the church bells in the area. On quiet days—though those are rare in Rome—the sound can be heard on Esquiline Hill over 2 miles (3 km) away. But climbing Janiculum Hill to witness the spectacle is a worthwhile trip. The panoramic views are explosive!

The Order of Malta is the oldest lasting order of knights in the world.

SNEAK PEEK

One of the best views in Rome is hiding in a secret keyhole on Aventine Hill! You might have learned that it's rude to peek through keyholes, but you can break the rules for this one. Pass the Garden of Oranges and find the door of the **Institute of the Order of Malta**. (The line of people waiting to peep will give it away.) Press your eye against the tiny window for a perfect picture of the dome of St. Peter's Basilica in the distance, framed by lush garden hedges.

FRIES, A SHAKE, AND...

If you're catching a train at **Termini station** and are hankering for a snack, go to the McDonald's on the basement level—your meal will come with a side of ruins! Builders discovered this well-preserved section of the Servian Wall during construction. Roughly 2,000 years ago, it was built to protect Rome against its invading neighbors. Ruins of the wall can also be found outside the Termini station, the Colosseum, and the Roman Forum.

> Ancient Romans invented an early version of concrete. It was made with a mixture of volcanic ash, lime, and water.

HAIR-RAISING DOLLS

The **Ospedale delle Bambole** (Doll Hospital) is also sometimes called "the shop of terror" because, well, the piles of doll heads, limbs, and bodies stacked in the window are a little creepy. Those brave enough to enter this tiny store are rewarded with a one-of-a-kind experience. Here, skilled craftspeople repair broken antique dolls to give them new life. Occasionally, lucky visitors will be treated to a doll-repair demonstration!

IMAGES: A section of the Servian Wall preserved in Termini station (above); the Doll Hospital window display (right); the daily cannon firing from Janiculum Hill (opposite top); peeking through the keyhole on Aventine Hill (opposite bottom).

TIME TO GO

P-U-TIFUL SEWER

Of all Rome's epic achievements, the *Cloaca Maxima* could be the smelliest. First built as a drainage ditch at the marshy Roman Forum, it was one of the world's first sewer systems. Nicknamed the Great Sewer, the cloaca handled some water waste from public baths and latrines, but its main job was to direct natural stormwater and flows from the aqueducts. You can visit the **Ponte Rotto** to see a trickle of water where it exits the tunnel system. There is also a sewer door near the Roman Forum, close to the Basilica Julia. Lean close to hear the sounds of softly running water inside—and sniff if you dare!

TOILET TOOLS

Historians believe that ancient Romans would wipe with a *xylospongium*, a simple tool fashioned with a sea sponge attached to a wooden stick. Like the toilet bench, this tool was likely shared! Another possibility is that the stick sponge was used as a toilet brush. Hopefully, it wasn't both!

In 2012, a robot was sent into the stinky tunnels to assess the condition of the ancient structure.

CURIOUS COMMODES

Ancient Romans knew how to take care of business. Yes, even that business. In addition to their ornate bathhouses, sewers, and aqueducts, Romans had *foricae*—public toilets. Imagine holes evenly spaced along a long bench. And forget the stall doors: public toilets could be shared by dozens of people at a time, sitting cheek-to-cheek! Waste would be "flushed" through gutters underneath the benches. If you have to see it to believe it, visit the ruins of the archaeological site **Ostia Antica**, where you will find a well-preserved example of an early restroom.

IMAGES: A view of the Cloaca Maxima from Palatine Bridge (above); ruins of ancient toilets at Ostia Antica (left).

Secrets of the City 129

WHAT'S THE DIFFERENCE?

The Spanish Steps are one of Rome's most famous attractions. Can you spot the five differences between these two pictures? See answers on page 140.

WHAT'S THE DIFFERENCE?

Dolphins and dragons adorn this beautiful fountain on Piazza Navona. Can you spot the five differences between these two pictures? See answers on page 140.

INDEX

A

al fresco (outdoor) dining **58–59**, 60, **60**
Al Sogno (toy store) 36
Altare della Patria monument **84–85**
amusement parks 40–41, **40–41**
Apollo and Daphne (statue) 92, **92**
Appia Antica Park 74, 116–117, **116–117**
Appian Way (Via Appia) 22, **22–23**, 28, 74–75, **74–75**, 116
Aqueduct Park 116–117, **116–117**
aqueducts **74–75**, 86, **86**, 87, 116–117, **116–117**
Arch of Constantine **15**, **28–29**
archaeological sites
    ancient toilets 128–129, **128–129**
    metro stations 27, **27**
    Palazzo Valentini 39
    Servian Wall 127, **127**
    Vicus Caprarius 87, **87**
art museums. *See* museums
art nouveau 90, **90**
automobiles 24, **24**, 30–31, **30–31**
Aventine Hill 48, 49, 126, **126**

B

Barcaccia Fountain 87, **87**
Basilica of San Crisogono 125, **125**
Basilica of St. Mary in Cosmedin 123, **123**
Basilica San Clemente 48
Baths of Caracalla **15**, 34–35, **34–35**
beaches 112, **112–113**, **141**
Bernini, Gian Lorenzo 52, 92, 97, 119, 121
Bernini, Pietro 87
biking **8–9**, **21**, 108, 113
Bioparco **15**, 100–101, **100–101**
birds 104–105, **104–105**, 109, 113
boars 102, **102**
boating 109, **109**, 113
Bocca della Verità (Mouth of Truth) 123, **123**
"Bone Chapel" (Capuchin Crypt) 56–57, **56–57**
Borromini, Francesco 120
Botanical Garden (Orto Botanico) **14**, 114–115, **114–115**
Botteghiamo Project **84**
Bruno, Giordano 111
buses 25, **25**

C

cabs 24, **24**
Caesar, Julius 24, 54
Campo de Fiori market **110–111**, 111
Capitoline Hill 48
Capitoline Museums 52, **52**

Capitoline wolf statue 48, **49**
Capuchin Crypt ("Bone Chapel") 56–57, **56–57**
Carriage Pavilion, Vatican Museums 22
cars 24, **24**, 30–31, **30–31**
Casina delle Civette (The House of Owls) **15**, 91, **91**
Casina di Raffaello 109, **109**
Castel di Guido Reserve 96
Castel Sant'Angelo **14**, 34–35, **34–35**
Catacombs of Rome 56–57, **56–57**, **74–75**, 75
Catacombs of San Callisto **74–75**, 75
cats 98–99, **98–99**, 114, **114–115**
Centrale Montemartini 53, **53**
Centro Storico (Historic Center) 12, 16, **16–17**, 67, **67**, 76–77, **76–77**
Chiesa di Sant'Eusebio 98
Church of St. Ignazio 120, **120**
Cinema dei Piccoli 89, **89**, 91
Circo Massimo (Circus Maximus) 42–43, **42–43**, 110
Cloaca Maxima 128–129, **128–129**
Colosseum **8–9**, 12, **15**, **20–21**, 43, **70–71**, 80–81, **80–81**, 127
corner shrine (*edicola sacra*) 77
cycling **8–9**, **21**, 108, 113

D

da Vinci, Leonardo 38, 93
Doll Hospital (Ospedale delle Bambole) 127, **127**

E

edicola sacra (corner shrine) 77
electric tuk tuk 25, **25**
Emmanuel II, King 55
Esquiline Hill 48, 126
"The Eternal City" nickname 13
Explora (children's museum) 38, **38**

F

farmers markets 110–111, **110–111**
Farnese Gardens **17**
Ferrovie Urbane (Urban Railway) 27, **27**
festivals 45, **45**
Flaminio Obelisk 36, 37, **37**
food 58–69
    al fresco (outdoor) dining **58–59**, 60, **60**
    ancient Rome 60, 61, 62, 64, 67
    bucatini all'amatriciana 63, **63**
    cacio e pepe 63, **63**
    carbonara 62, **62**
    chocolatier 84
    courses 60
    "fifth quarter" (organ meats) 61, **61**

134   A Kid's Guide to ROME

fried artichokes 65, **65**
gelato 68, **68**
grattachecca (icy treat) 69, **69**
iconic eateries 66–67, **66–67**
Jewish Quarter 45, **45**, 65, **65**
paninis 67
panino con porchetta (roasted pork sandwich) 65, **65**
panna cotta 69, **69**
pasta 62–63, **62–63**
pastry shops 67, **67**
pecorino romano cheese 61, **61**
pizza 66, **66**
sandwiches 65, **65**, 67, **67**
street food 64–65, **64–65**
supplì 64, **64**
tiramisu 68, **68**
foot statue 55, **55**
Foro Italico (sports complex) 42–43, **42–43**
Fountain of the Bees 97
foxes **94–95**, 103, **103**

G
Galleria Alberto Sordi **82–83**, 84
Galleria Borghese 52, **52**, 92, **92**
Galleria Sciarra 90, **90**
gardens. *See* parks and gardens
gelato 68, **68**
Giardino del Lago 109, **109**
Gladiator School 89, **89**
gladiators 81, **81**, 89
golf-cart tours 25
Great Synagogue (Tempio Maggiore) 45
gulls 104, **104**

H
Hadrian, Emperor 34
herring gulls 104, **104**
hills 12, 29, 48–49, **48–49**, 126, **126**
Historic Center (Centro Storico) 12, 16, **16–17**, 67, **67**, 76–77, **76–77**
The House of Owls (Casina delle Civette) **15**, 91, **91**
Hydromania (water park) 40–41, **40–41**

I
IKONO Roma 39, **39**
Il Vittoriano ("the typewriter") monument 77
Institute of the Order of Malta 126, **126**
Isola Tiberina (Tiber Island) 44, **44**
Italian phrases 10

J
Janiculum Hill 126, **126**
Jesus Christ 28
Jewish Quarter 45, **45**, 65, 67
Julius II, Pope 79

K
Keats, John 73, 114
knights 126

L
La Campana (restaurant) 66, **66**
language 10
Lateran Basilica 125, **125**
Leonardi, Francesco 63
Leonardo da Vinci 38, 93
Limited Traffic Zone (ZTL) 24, **24**
LunEur (amusement park) 40–41, **40–41**
Lungo il Tevere 45, **45**

M
maps **14–19**
Marble Foot Way (Via del Piè di Marmo) 55, **55**
Marcus Aurelias, Emperor 54, **54**
markets 64, 110–111, **110–111**
Mercato Trionfale 110
metro 18–19, **18–19**, 27, **27**
Michelangelo 29, 51, 93
milestones 23, **23**
Monte Mario 50
Monti neighborhood 16, 66
motorbikes 30–31, **30–31**
Mouth of Truth (Bocca della Verità) 123, **123**
museums
    Capitoline Museums 52, **52**
    Carriage Pavilion 22
    Centrale Montemartini 53, **53**
    Explora (children's museum) 38, **38**
    Galleria Borghese 52, **52**, 92, **92**
    IKONO Roma 39, **39**
    Museo Civico di Zoologia 100–101, **100–101**
    Museo Mostra di Leonardo 38, **38**
    Museum of Illusions **15**, 121, **121**
    Ostia Antica 112, **128–129**, 129
    Palazzo Massimo alle Terme 53, **53**
    Piaggio Museum 30
    Vatican Museums 22, **78–79**, 79, 93, **93**
    Welcome to Rome 39, **39**

N
nasoni ("big noses") drinking fountains 86, **86**
Neve Di Latte 68
nutria 103, **103**

O

obelisks 36, 37, **37**, 42
opera 88, **88**
Orange Garden **106–107**
Order of Malta 126, **126**
Orto Botanico (Botanical Garden) **14**, 114–115, **114–115**
Ospedale delle Bambole (Doll Hospital) 127, **127**
Ostia 112, **112–113**, 141, **141**
Ostia Antica 112, **128–129**, 129

P

Palatine Hill 48, **48–49**, 49
Palazzo Massimo alle Terme 53, **53**
Palazzo Spada 120, **120**
Palazzo Valentini 39
Pantheon **14**, 72, **72**, 76
parakeets 105, **105**
parks and gardens
    Appia Antica Park 74, 116–117, **116–117**
    Aqueduct Park 116–117, **116–117**
    Casina di Raffaello 109, **109**
    Farnese Gardens **17**
    Giardino del Lago 109, **109**
    LunEur amusement park 40–41, **40–41**
    Orange Garden **106–107**
    Orto Botanico (Botanical Garden) 114–115, **114–115**
    Parco Adriano 34
    Tor di Quinto Park 113
    Vatican Gardens 78
    Villa Borghese 108, **108**
    water parks **32–33**, 40–41, **40–41**
pasta 62–63, **62–63**
pastry shops 67, **67**
pecorino romano cheese 61, **61**
peregrine falcons 104, **104**
Peri, Jacopo 88
Piaggio Ape (mini trucks) 30
Piaggio Museum 30
Piazza del Campidoglio **28–29**, 29, 48, **49**, 54, **54**, 97
Piazza del Popolo 36–37, **36–37**, 42, 84, 85, 109
Piazza di Spagna 87, **87**
Piazza Navona **14**, 36, 76
Piazza San Giovanni 42
Piazza Venezia 84, **84–85**, 85
Pinocchio 91
Pius IX, Pope 53, 126
pizza 66, **66**
playgrounds and play centers 34, 109, **109**
Ponte Fabricio 44
Ponte Rotto 128–129, **128–129**
Ponte Sant'Angelo 51, **51**
Ponte Umberto 51
popes
    death 124, 125
    fortress 35
    as head of church and Holy See 78
    hearts on display 124
    Julius II 79
    pasta for 63
    Pius IX 53, 126
    popemobile 30, **30**, 53
    smoke signal announcing new pope 78
    Sylvester II 125
    tombs 75, 125, **125**
    Vatican Museums and 79, 93
Porta Alchemica 123, **123**
Porta Maggiore 26
Pozzo, Andrea 120
Prati neighborhood 16, **26**
Protestant Cemetery 73, 114–115, **114–115**
puppet theater 91, **91**
Pyramid of Caius Cestius 98, 115, **115**

Q

Quartiere Coppedè neighborhood 122, **122**

R

Raphael 93
red foxes **94–95**, 103, **103**
Regoli Pasticceria 67, **67**
Remus and Romulus 48, 49, 96
restaurants. *See* food
rioni (districts) **16–17**
roads
    ancient Roman builders 22, 23
    Appian Way 22, **22–23**, 28, 74–75, **74–75**, 116
    unusual rides 30–31, **30–31**
    Zona Traffico Limitado (ZTL) 24, **24**
Roman Forum *12–13*, **15**, **17**, **48–49**, 49, 127
Romulus and Remus 48, 49, 96

S

SAID (chocolatemaker) 84
San Carlino Puppet Theater 91, **91**
San Cosimato 110
San Lorenzo neighborhood 55, **55**
sandwiches 65, **65**, 67, **67**
Santi Vincenzo e Anastasio 124, **124**
Scala Sancta 28
The School of Athens (Raphael painting) 93, **93**
sculptures 52–55, **52–55**
Servian Wall 127, **127**
Seven Hills of Rome 12, 29, 48–49, **48–49**, 126, **126**
sewer system 128–129, **128–129**
Shelley, Percy Bysshe 114
shopping 36, 64, 110–111, **110–111**
Sistine Chapel 78, 79, 93, **93**
Spanish Steps 73, **73**
sports
    Circo Massimo (Circus Maximus) 42–43, **42–43**
    Foro Italico (sports complex) 42–43, **42–43**
    Ostia swimming 112, **112–113**
    Stadio Olimpico del Nuoto (Olympic Swimming Stadium) 42
    water park **32–33**, 40–41, **40–41**
St. Anthony 98

St. Peter's Basilica **14**, **46–47**, 51, **51**, **78–79**, **126**
St. Peter's Square **16**, **51**, 98, **118–119**, 121, **121**
starlings 105, **105**
street food 64-65, **64–65**
subway 18–19, **18–19**, 27, **27**
swimming
    Ostia 112, **112–113**
    Stadio Olimpico del Nuoto (Olympic Swimming
      Stadium) 42
    water park **32–33**, 40-41, **40–41**
Sylvester II, Pope 125

T
Taigi, Anna Maria 125, **125**
taxis 24, **24**
Teatro dell'Opera 88, **88**
Tempio Maggiore (the Great Synagogue) 45
Temple of Aesculapius 109, **109**
Termini station **27**, 127, **127**
Testaccio Market 64, 110
Tiber Island (Isola Tiberina) 44, **44**
Tiber River
    facts 112
    floods 87
    Lungo il Tevere festival 45, **45**
    Lungotevere (river waterfront) **112–113**, 113
    on map **14**
    Ostia's beaches 112, **112–113**
    Romulus and Remus in 96
    Tiber Island (Isola Tiberina) 44-45, **44–45**
    wildlife 101, 103, **103**
tiramisu 68, **68**
toilets 128-129, **128–129**
Tor di Quinto Park 113
Torre Argentina Cat Sanctuary 98, **98–99**
traffic 24
trains 18–19, **18–19**, 27, **27**, 112
trams 26, **26**
Trastevere neighborhood **14**, 16, 26, 66, 110, 114–115,
   114–115
Trevi Fountain 12, **15**, 73, **73**, 86
trompe l'oeil 120-121, **120–121**
Turtle Fountain 97
"the typewriter" (Il Vittoriano) monument 77
Tyrrhenian Sea 112, 141, **141**

U
Urban Railway (Ferrovie Urbane) 27, **27**

V
Vatican City
    about 78
    on map **14**, **16**
    secret tunnels 35
    Sistine Chapel 78, 79, 93, **93**
    St. Peter's Basilica **14**, **46–47**, 51, **51**, **78–79**, **126**
    St. Peter's Square **16**, **51**, 98, **118–119**, 121, **121**
    Vatican Gardens 78

Vatican Museums 22, **78–79**, 79, 93, **93**
Vespa **30–31**, 31
Via Appia (Appian Way) 22, **22–23**, 28, 74-75,
   74–75, 116
Via dei Fori Imperiali 54
Via del Corso 84-85, **84–85**
Via del Piè di Marmo (Marble Foot Way) 55, **55**
Via Tiburtina 84
Via Veneto 57
Viale dei Bambini 91, 109
Viale del Lago trail 109
Vicus Caprarius 87, **87**
Villa Ada 108
Villa Borghese
    Bioparco (zoo) **15**, 100-101, **100–101**
    Casina di Raffaello 109, 109
    Cinema dei Piccoli 89, **89**, 91
    Galleria Borghese 52, **52**, 92, **92**
    on map **14**
    park 108, **108**
    sculpted dragons and water horses 97
    water clock 109, **109**
Villa Doria Pamphilj 103, 108
Villa Torlonia 91
Virgil (poet) 13
Il Vittoriano ("the typewriter") monument 77

W
water parks **32–33**, 40-41, **40–41**
Welcome to Rome 39, **39**
What's the difference? **130–133**, **140**
wild boars 102, **102**
wildlife 94-105, **94–105**
wolves 96-97, **96–97**

Z
Zodiac Terrace 50, **50**
Zona Traffico Limitado (ZTL) 24, **24**
zoo **15**, 100-101, **100–101**
Zuccari Palace 122, **122**

Index 137

RESOURCES & PHOTO CREDITS

Getting Around Town (pages 20-31)
ATAC Rome: atac.roma.it/en

Places to Play (pages 32-45)
Castel Sant'Angelo: castelsantangelo.com
Explora Children's Museum: mdbr.it
Hydromania: hydromania.it
IKONO Roma: ikono.global
LunEur Park: luneurpark.it
Lungo il Tevere Summer Festival:
    lungoiltevereroma.it
Museo Mostra di Leonardo: mostradileonardo.com
Stadio Olimpico: asroma.com
Welcome to Rome: welcometo-rome.it

What a View! (pages 46-57)
Borghese Gallery & Museum: galleriaborghese.
    beniculturali.it
Capitoline Museums: museicapitolini.org
Capuchin Crypt: museoecriptacappuccini.it
Centrale Montemartini: centralemontemartini.org
Santa Maria Sopra Minerva:
    santamariasopraminerva.it
St. Peter's Basilica: basilicasanpietro.va

Let's Eat! (pages 58-69)
Neve di Latte: nevedilatte.it
Pasticceria Regoli: pasticceriaregoli.com
Pecorino Romano Cheese Consortium (DOP):
    pecorinoromano.com
Testaccio Market: mercatoditestaccio.it
Trapizzino: trapizzino.it

Hub of History (pages 70-81)
Colosseum: thecolosseum.org
Vatican Museums: museivaticani.va

Modern Marvels (pages 82-93)
Cinema dei Piccoli: cinemadeipiccoli.com
Galleria Alberto Sordi: galleriaalbertosordi.com
Rome Gladiator School: romegladiatorschool.com
Said chocolate factory: said.it
Vicus Caprarius: vicuscaprarius.com

The Wild Side (pages 94-105)
Bioparco: bioparco.it
Museo Civico di Zoologia: museocivicodizoologia.it
Torre Argentina Cat Sanctuary: gattidiroma.net

Going Green (pages 106-117)
Appia Antica Park: parcoappiaantica.it
Orto Botanico: ortobotanicodiroma.it
The Protestant Cemetery: cemeteryrome.it

Secrets of the City (pages 118-129)
Museum of Illusions: moiroma.it
Ostia Antica: ostiaantica.beniculturali.it

138   A Kid's Guide to ROME

IMAGE CREDITS

Illustrations © 2025 John Foster
8-9: Jon Bower at Apexphotos/Getty Images / **12-13:** Patryk_Kosmider/Getty Images / **16-17:** Jupiterimages/Getty Images (St. Peter's Square); Hercules Milas/Alamy Stock Photo (Domus Augustana); iStockphoto/Getty Images (Farnese Gardens); Mustang_79/Getty Images (Roman Forum) / **18-19:** Phuong D. Nguyen/Shutterstock (people in metro station); Alexandros Michailidis/Shutterstock (metro platform); bbbrrn/Getty Images (metro sign) / **20-21:** TFILM/Getty Images / **22-23:** ValerioMei/Shuttestock (Appian Way); Tatsuo Nakamura/Shutterstock (milestone) / **24-25:** sandrixroma/Getty Images (ZTL sign); pedro emanuel pereira/Getty Images (cabs); flavijus/Getty Images (buses); NOWRA photography/Shutterstock (tuk-tuk) / **26-27:** rarrarorro/Getty Images (tram); Sergey-73/Shutterstock (Termini station); REPORT/Shutterstock (metro relics) / **28-29:** Justin Foulkes/Lonely Planet (Piazza del Campidoglio); Dominika Zarzycka/SOPA Images/LightRocket via Getty Images (Arch of Constantine) / **30-31:** Jupiterimages/Getty Images (mini car); bluesky85/Getty Images (popemobile); Jarek Pawlak/Shutterstock (Vespa) / **32-33:** MZeta/Shutterstock / **34-35:** Danny Lehman/Getty Images (Castel Sant'Angelo); Wirestock/istock / Getty Images (Baths of Caracalla) / **36-37:** Anton Aleksenko/Getty Images / **38-39:** Martin Moos/Lonely Planet (*Explora*); Janaka Dharmasena/Shutterstock (drawing); ChrisDoAI/Getty Images (ball pit); Michael Blann/Getty Images (theater seats) / **40-41:** MZeta/Shutterstock (water park); Stefano Tammaro/Shutterstock (LunEur) / **42-43:** Aerial-motion/Shutterstock (Foro Italico); mikroman6/Getty Images (Circo Massimo) / **44-45:** ROMAOSLO/Getty Images (Tiber Island); Photo Beto/iStock (Jewish Quarter); Elizabeth Beard/Getty Images (Lungo il Tevere) / **46-47:** iStockphoto/Getty Images / **48-49:** iStockphoto/Getty Images (Roman Forum); Angelika Stern/Getty Images (wolf statue) / **50-51:** essevu/Shutterstock (Zodiac Terrace); r.nagy/Shutterstock (Ponte Sant'Angelo); f11photo/Shutterstock (St. Peter's Basilica view) / **52-53:** Viacheslav Lopatin/Shutterstock (busts); wjarek/Shutterstock (Bernini sculptures); River Thompson/Lonely Planet (statue); LPETTET/Getty Images (coins) / **54-55:** John Harper/Getty Images (Marcus Aurelius statue); liberowolf/Shutterstock (marble foot); Stefano Tammaro/Shutterstock (street art) / **56-57:** FILIPPO MONTEFORTE/AFP via Getty Images (Roman catacombs); Richard Ross/Getty Images (Capuchin Crypt) / **58-59:** Imgorthand/Getty Images / **60-61:** Kirk Fisher/Shutterstock (kids playing); Nico Tondini/Getty Images (*coratella*); barmalini/Getty Images (*pecorino*) / **62-63:** Sea Wave/Shutterstock (carbonara); AlexPro9500/Getty Images (*cacio e pepe*); EzumeImages/Getty Images (bucatini) / **64-65:** Marzia Giacobbe/Getty Images (*suppli*); piola666/Getty Images (*porchetta* sandwich); Fabrizio Esposito/Shutterstock (artichokes) / **66-67:** Catarina Belova/Shutterstock (*ristorante*); AndreyPopov/Getty Images (pizza); CFEDEph/Shutterstock (focaccia sandwich); Alexandra Bruzzese/Lonely Planet (*pasticceria*) / **68-69:** New Africa/Shutterstock (tiramisu); nelea33/Shutterstock (*panna cotta*); Alexandra Bruzzese/Lonely Planet (gelato); Stefano Carocci Ph/Shutterstock (icy treat) / **70-71:** by Ruhey/Getty Images / **72-73:** iStockphoto/Getty Images (Pantheon); S.Borisov/Shutterstock (Spanish Steps); fazon1/Getty Images (Trevi Fountain) / **74-75:** Danut Vieru/Shutterstock (aqueduct); Sun_Shine/Shutterstock (catacombs gate) / **76-77:** poludziber/Shutterstock (Centro Storico); Bernard Bialorucki/Getty Images (*edicola sacra*) / **78-79:** Mariia Golovianko/Shutterstock (St. Peter's Square); Chanclos/Shutterstock (statue) / **80-81:** scaliger/Getty Images (Colosseum); Stefano Bianchetti/Corbis via Getty Images (engraving); Jin Mamengni/Xinhua via Getty Images (*hypogeum*) / **82-83:** F8 studio/Shutterstock / **84-85:** ValerioMei/Shutterstock / **86-87:** LUIS PADILLA-Fotografia/Shutterstock (aqueduct); MNStudio/Shutterstock (*nasone*); Kirk Fisher/Shutterstock (Vicus Caprarius); Matteo Colombo/Getty Images (Baraccia Fountain) / **88-89:** polya_olya/Shutterstock (opera house); ANDREAS SOLARO/AFP via Getty Images (Gladiator School); Massimo Salesi/Shutterstock (Cinema dei Piccoli) / **90-91:** Only Fabrizio/Shutterstock (Galleria Sciarra); Phant/Shutterstock (Casina delle Civette); Yuri Turkov/Alamy Stock Photo (puppet theater) / **92-93:** Paolo Gallo/Shutterstock (*Apollo and Daphne*); Viacheslav Lopatin/Shutterstock (*The School of Athens*); Creative Lab/Shutterstock (Sistine Chapel) / **94-95:** Photographer shooting: Architecture, Black&White, Landscapes, Nature, Outdoor, Portraits, Video/Getty Images / **96-97:** ValerioMei/Shutterstock / **98-99:** Kirk Fisher/Shutterstock (tabby cat); Thierry Monasse/Getty Images (cat sanctuary) / **100-101:** Gianluca Rasile/Shutterstock (lion); Giorgio Cosulich de Pecine/Getty Images (taxidermy) / **102-103:** Dario Pautasso/Shutterstock (wild boar); LauraDinca/Shutterstock (fox); Half65/Shutterstock (nutria) / **104-105:** YKD/Shutterstock (gull); Traxparent Wildlife/Shutterstock (peregrine falcon); gergosz/Shutterstock (parakeet); Francesco Todaro/Shutterstock (starlings) / **106-107:** nomadFra/Shutterstock /

108-109: Kamira/Shutterstock (fountains); ValerioMei/Getty Images (lake); ncristian/Shutterstock (water clock) / **110-111:** Jon Lovette/Getty Images / **112-113:** Zakhar Mar/Shutterstock (beach); ValerioMei/Shutterstock (river path) / **114-115:** Alina La Cat/Shutterstock (cat on headstone); Aleksandr Medvedkov/Shutterstock (pyramid); ValerioMei/Shutterstock (Orto Botanico) / **116-117:** Jannis Tobias Werner/Shutterstock (Via Appia Antica); sandrixroma/Shutterstock (Aqueduct Park) / **118-119:** Geert Smet/Shutterstock / **120-121:** Anna Pakutina/Shutterstock (Church of St. Ignazio); essevu/Shutterstock (Palazzo Spada); OttoPles/Shutterstock (colonnades); Svetlana_Smirnova/Shutterstock (optical illusion) / **122-123:** Vlas Telino studio/Shutterstock (Quartiere Coppedè); ValerioMei/Shutterstock (Zuccari Palace); E. O./Shutterstock (Porta Alchemica); Sorin Colac/Shutterstock (Mouth of Truth) / **124-125:** Alexnow/Getty Images (Santi Vincenzo e Anastasio); David Henley/Pictures from History/Universal Images Group via Getty Images (Basilica di San Crisogono); Zoran Karapancev/Shutterstock (Lateran Basilica) / **126-127:** Photo by Massimo Valicchia/NurPhoto via Getty Images (cannon); Matteo Gabrieli/Shutterstock (keyhole); adam eastland/Alamy Stock Photo (Servian Wall); Education Images/Universal Images Group via Getty Images (Doll Hospital) / **128-129:** Lucamato/Shutterstock (Cloaca Maxima); Claudio Morini/Shutterstock (toilets) / **130-131:** Nicola Forenza/Shutterstock / **132-133:** Givaga/Getty Images / **141:** DedMityay/Shutterstock

WHAT'S THE DIFFERENCE? ANSWERS

Ostia is the only Roman district located on the Tyrrhenian Sea. Through Rome's history, it has served as a military base and an important trade port.